PRAISE

FOR

The Ta Ta Weenie Club

"Bill Torrey is a natural storyteller who's had the advantage of growing up on a farm, a setting full of stories. By turns wacky, hilarious, or heart wrenching, *The Ta Ta Weenie Club* will have you reaching for Bill's tales for years to come, and trying out some unique Vermont expressions that you've probably never heard before."

—Willem Lange

"Bill Torrey's laugh-out-loud tales of his childhood in Vermont ring more true than any I have read. If you want to know the real Vermont, don't miss this wonderful collection. It's a long-gone Vermont, seen and lived through the eyes of a young Vermonter growing up in it. "

—Bill Schubart, author of *I Am Baybie*

7/10/17

BILL TORREY

❧

THE TA TA

WEENIE

CLUB

GREEN WRITERS PRESS

Brattleboro, Vermont

Printed in the United States

10 9 8 7 6 5 4 3 2 1

Green Writers Press is a Vermont-based publisher whose mission is
to spread a message of hope and renewal through the words and
images we publish. Throughout we will adhere to our commitment to
preserving and protecting the natural resources of the earth. To that
end, a percentage of our proceeds will be donated to environmental
activist groups. Green Writers Press gratefully acknowledges support
from individual donors, friends, and readers to help support the
environment and our publishing initiative.

Green
writers
press

Giving Voice to Writers & Artists Who Will Make the World a Better Place
Green Writers Press | Brattleboro, Vermont
www.greenwriterspress.com

ISBN: 978-0997452808

For more information, visit the author's website:
www.billtorrey.com

PRINTED ON PAPER WITH PULP THAT COMES FROM FSC-CERTIFIED FORESTS, MANAGED FORESTS
THAT GUARANTEE RESPONSIBLE ENVIRONMENTAL, SOCIAL, AND ECONOMIC PRACTICES BY
LIGHTNING SOURCE. ALL WOOD PRODUCT COMPONENTS USED IN BLACK & WHITE, STANDARD
COLOR, OR SELECT COLOR PAPERBACK BOOKS, UTILIZING EITHER CREAM OR WHITE BOOKBLOCK
PAPER, THAT ARE MANUFACTURED IN THE LAVERGNE, TENNESSEE PRODUCTION CENTER ARE
SUSTAINABLE FORESTRY INITIATIVE® (SFI®) CERTIFIED SOURCING.

To Wendy Andersen for her vast wisdom and quiet advice.
To Terry Cleveland for her never-ending encouragement.
To Karen for her steady devotion and unlimited patience.
I'm a long shot honey, but they do come in.

Grandson James. Ta Ta Weenie-In-Training.

CONTENTS

"Some make saints, some make sinners.

Big fish grow from little minners"

—Francis Colburn

〜

～

INTRODUCTION

I was born and raised in Vermont during the '60s and early
'70s. My siblings and I weathered the storm of adolescence
without X-boxes, Nintendos, Play Stations, computers, and
cell phones. We didn't have the Internet and 150 channels on
TV. We had three channels on a good clear day, and mostly
in black and white. Oh, they were broadcasting in color. But
my dad wouldn't buy a color set until he figured they had the
technology perfected. That turned out to be about ten years.

When my mother brought one of us kids to the doctor,
and the examination was over, they would sit and chat while
each of them smoked a cigarette. My siblings and I were
yanked out of my mother with forceps while my father sat in
the designated waiting area. There weren't birthing centers
and Lamaze classes.

They brought us home to our lead-base-painted bed-
rooms and placed us on our bellies in cribs that could fold up

like a bear trap. There weren't childproof caps on medicine bottles, drain cleaner, or antifreeze. We didn't have car seats, seat belts, or airbags. Riding in the back of my dad's pickup was a common occurrence, and something we called dibs on.

We ate real butter on white bread. We ate sausage, ham, bacon, and eggs. We wolfed down burgers, hot dogs, steaks, pork chops, roast pork, and roast beef, side-dressed with piles of potatoes and gravy, or home-fries with ketchup. For desserts we had cookies, pies, doughnuts, cakes, fudge, and ice cream. We drank Kool-Aid by the barrel, made with tons of sugar. And my siblings and I were in the best shape of our lives. There wasn't one fat kid among us.

We had family, friends, and neighbors, and we went outside and did things with them. We entertained ourselves by doing things that involved physical activity. I could leave the house in the morning and be home by dusk, and nobody would issue an Amber Alert.

We had jumps and trails for our bikes, sleds, and saucers. We played baseball, football, basketball, dodge ball, kickball, toss and catch, flys and grounders, freeze tag, red rover, and hide-and-seek.

We made stuff. We made tunnels in the hay mow and snowbanks. Built tree forts and snow forts. We made swings from rafters, trees, and vines. We climbed trees just for the fun of it. We went hunting and fishing. We rode our bikes, horses, ponies, and even pigs and cows.

We got in apple fights (those sting!), snowball fights, mudball fights, cow-flop fights (you have to get damn close to someone to hit 'em with a dry cow flop, they just don't fly far), and even some fistfights.

We had knives, hatchets, BB guns, bows and arrows, sling-shots, and spears, and nobody put an eye out. We broke a few bones, got scraped, scratched, cut, bruised, banged up, and knocked down.

We got spanked. With wooden spoons, spatulas, rulers, paddles, belts, and switches. And nobody got sued or called child protection services. If you got in trouble at school, you got in more trouble when you got home.

What lies ahead are stories of a time and place that was a wonderful sort of limbo. A space between country and urban life that has evaporated into the fog of progress hailed by some as a blessing and by others as a blight. Supermarkets with products from far and wide were becoming all the rage, yet we grew our own vegetables and raised our own grass-fed beef. Not because it was the latest trend. We just couldn't afford not to.

My parents loved and respected each other and raised us under the umbrella of that love and respect. They taught us right from wrong. There was a time to work and a time to play. My Mom and Dad could go out dancing and drinking on a Saturday night and to church on Sunday morning without any guilt or regrets for doing either.

I grew up with freedom. Freedom to roam the woods and fields, and play in a real and wholesome place. Freedom to fail, and freedom to succeed. The freedom to learn respect and responsibility. Freedom for adventure. I learned how to cope with all of it. I ran through it, rode through it, walked, crawled, and sneaked through it. Became the man I am. These are some of the tales of those adventures.

~

Little Garth

We always had seven or eight beef cows when I was a kid. The first type we had were Black Angus, but after a couple years we got rid of them. We phased them out of the pasture and into the freezer and switched to Herefords. We did this for a couple of reasons. The first one was because they were like wild buffaloes and were always busting out of the pasture, and it was usually at night. Which brings us to the second reason. They were black.

There was one summer night when those Black Angus got out in the road and I was helping to put them back in. I was around nine years old. My Old Man gave me the plumb assignment of blocking the road and turning them into the gate that was swung open while he and a couple of my older siblings went to hunt them down and chase them my way.

I'm standing there on Route 117 in the pitch dark when suddenly I hear the pounding of hooves on pavement coming

7

towards me. Getting closer. Then I hear this wild bellowing. It ain't the cows. It's my dad running behind them, yelling "STOP THEM, TURN 'EM!"

But they were BLACK! I couldn't see them! And even worse, I figured they couldn't see me. I jumped up on the back side of the gate and waved my arms at them like a wash on a windy day. I caught just a brief glimpse of them as they blasted by me down the road. Mostly just the whites of their eyes.

And if you think it was difficult to get them back into the pasture, it didn't hold a candle to trying to get them into a cattle truck when it came time to have them fitted with freezer paper. It was like watching a poorly run rodeo without horses, just clowns.

Our cows were for the most part untamed and skiddish of human contact because nobody ever made the effort or took the time to learn them otherwise. But there was one cow though, that was given the time and attention to learn of the bond that can build when kindness is given. The relationship started one February day in 1967.

It was downright frigid the afternoon I found the little calf out in the barnyard while I was helping my dad do the chores. His nose was blue and he was barely breathing. His mother wouldn't have anything to do with him. It was her first calf and she just didn't know what to do. My dad did though.

"We've got to get him warmed up soon, or his chances are slim to none," my Old Man said as he carried the calf back to the house. He brought the newborn down the hatchway into the cellar and laid him next to the wood stove.

Mom got me some clean rags to wash him with. The little red-and-white calf was trembling like a wet terrier in a cold wind as I scrubbed him with the warm rags. I was still rubbing him dry when the Old Man went outside to the dog kennel and brought our two rabbit hounds into the cellar to feed them supper.

The two beagles came over and sniffed at the calf. Smokey, the bluetick, started licking the little calf, just like his mother should have, and I kept fluffing him with the towels. And the calf started to perk up. After Ol' Smoke ate his chow, he went over and lay down just about on top of the calf and commenced licking him some more.

The Old Man had been watching us with a curious eye. "Let's leave Smokey in here with the calf for the night," he said. "Lord knows he hasn't amounted to much as a rabbit dog. Maybe he's better suited as a nursemaid."

It was a fact that the only rabbit the dog had ever interacted with was a half-grown cottontail. He'd brought it to the Old Man by the nape of the neck the way a mother dog would carry a pup: alive and unhurt. Dad had taken it from him and let it go under a brush pile.

Smokey curled right up next to the calf and slept with him through the night. And so did I. In the morning the calf stood up on shaky legs. The Old Man called his cattle dealer neighbor, Garth Perkins, and had him come over and give the calf a shot of antibiotic. That was how the calf got his name, Little Garth.

Garth Perkins was a man of considerable talents. From the Northeast Kingdom of Vermont, he had a native Yankee's accent and a sharp sense for business. He had been a logger, sawmill owner, pig farmer, dairy farmer, garbage man, cattle dealer, and probably more I didn't know of. He knew everybody in the county who was worth knowing, and most of the ones who weren't.

When it came to loading cows, Garth knew all the tricks to get the chosen victim into his cattle truck. And he could keep you laughing while you were damn near getting gored or trampled. I rode with my dad and Garth once in his cattle truck. We were taking three of our cows to a new pasture about five miles away up in Skunk Hollow.

When Garth dropped the ramp on the end of that truck, those cows piled out of there like the hounds of hell were nipping at their heels. They circled the meadow on a dead run, their tails straight up, looking for a break in the fence. Garth turned to the Old Man and said, "Let's get the hell out of here before they beat us home."

Little Garth became our only cow that was tame. I had to hand-feed him milk replacer for months. First from a big plastic bottle, then from a galvanized bucket with a big rubber teat down on the side of it. He and I got to know to each other. He'd follow me around like a big bovine dog whenever I was anywhere near him. He was good company.

Our land went from the Route 117, across railroad tracks, and all the way down to the Winooski River. As we had pasture across the tracks and because the tracks were gated and fenced in, we had to get some of our crazed cows across the tracks a few times each year. Doing so without us getting run down by our cows or the cows getting run down by the train was always an interesting challenge. Almost a sport.

Each spring, the Old Man would repair the river fence in the sections where the ice and high water had torn it up. While he did this, my brother George and I would fish. Mom made Dad tie us to a tree with baler twine. He would tether us with just enough twine so we could get our line into the water while we sat on a big rock. The day I caught my first perch I was hooked on fishing.

But I couldn't swim. Mom wouldn't let me fish the river unless I had somebody along who could save me if I fell in. Lining up somebody of that caliber on a regular basis was cramping my style. But I was scared of the water.

I finally found the courage and answer to my problem at the new community swimming pool a half a mile up the road. It offered swimming lessons, and I signed up. The lessons were at eight o'clock in the morning, rain or shine. I guess they figured you were going to get wet anyway. The water was freezing and the chlorine stung my eyes and left them bloodshot. I'd spend the rest of the day looking like a ten-year-old wino.

As soon as I passed the test to swim in the deep end, which involved swimming a lap of the pool and treading water, I was allowed to go fishing without supervision. And fish I did.

There was one minor hitch to fishing down back. His name was El Toro. El Toro was the bull my dad occasionally borrowed from Mr. Perkins to breed our cows. He was big and mean and had a set of horns that were fairly fearsome. They had about a four-foot spread from tip to tip and went straight out from the sides of his head.

The Old Man had told me not to fool around with him. He was very clear about it.

"You fool with that bull, and you'll get the horn up the ass." I was too young then to know what a metaphor was.

I vividly recall a spring day when my dad and I were walking across El Toro's pasture. He's was charging down on us like a bovine locomotive.

My dad leans over and says, "Don't move."

Like I was going to move! I was stuck to the side of his leg like a tick.

When El Toro got about thirty feet away, my dad threw up his arm like a hayseed traffic cop and shouts, "Stop right there!" And much to my amazement, El Toro pulled up and stopped right there. Dad took a step towards the bull and shouted, "Get the hell out of here!" And by God, El Toro got the hell out of there.

Dad turned to me and said, "Don't you ever run from him. You stand your ground and he'll back off."

Well, I thought, that's easy for him to say. He's so big and tall he could hunt geese with a long rake, and here I am, knee high to a short duck.

I admit that El Toro's ass was a choice target for my BB gun. Especially when I saw him knocking Little Garth around.

When Little Garth got older, the friendly steer had the unfortunate assignment of sharing the pasture with El Toro. Sharing wasn't a concept that had ever entered the old bull's skull. It was his pasture and his alone. I learned that the hard way one hot August day. That was the way I learned a lot of things in my youth.

Usually I'd take the longer path through the gully and stay out of sight of the bull. But not that day. That day I was preoccupied with my ongoing battle with Old Lead Pencil. He was the massive smallmouth bass that inhabited the stretch of river that I was steadily whipping into a froth with my fishing pole. I had briefly hooked and promptly lost the old monster the previous week.

Starting out through the pasture, I gave El Toro just a cursory glance. He was on the far side of his paddock and feeding contentedly. In hindsight, I believe his nonchalant grazing was just a ruse to get me within range. As soon as I got out into the middle of the pasture, his head shot up and he started walking my way, with Little Garth bringing up the rear.

I started walking a little faster and eyeballing the distance to the railroad fence up ahead. El Toro started to trot. I started to jog. He broke into a gallop. I broke into a sprint. I could hear my father's voice in my head saying, "Don't run!" But it was too late.

A railroad fence is about five feet tall and consist of ten-inch squares of steel wire that go all the way down to the ground. A body can't just roll under it quickly. It has to be climbed like a ladder right next to a post. All this is going through my head as I'm running towards the fence when it suddenly dawns on me: a tie at the fence is the same as a loss! So I did the only thing that I could do. What I knew I had to do.

I turned at the fence and faced El Toro. He's steaming down on me like a hairy freight train. I brandished my fishing pole as if it was a six-foot sword and I could parry the charging bull. I figured a pitiful display of courage to commemorate my last moments on this sweet earth would be appropriate.

And then Little Garth appeared. He came in sideways with a shoulder check that shoved El Toro to my right. The bull tossed his head and threw a wicked slash with his horns that just missed me as I jumped aside. It caught Little Garth right behind his front leg. The horn sank in damn near all the way. The steer staggered a couple steps and fell down.

El Toro bounced off the railroad fence and turned for another pass at me. Blood was dripping off his horn. I don't know why, but I wasn't scared anymore. I stood my ground.

Screaming as loud as I could, I whipped El Toro with the tip of my fishing pole on the soft skin of his nose. He was so close to me that I could smell his hot, rancid breath in my face.

He swapped ends to leave and I got two more licks in on his ass before he outran me. On the last swat, the treble hooks of the spinning lure on the end of my line got caught on the top of the bull's tail and the line snapped with a sharp crack. It was my favorite spinner.

I stood there blinking like an owl in the hot summer sun with sweat and tears running down my face.

"Come try it again, you red son of a bitch!" I screamed at him.

Then I remembered Little Garth. I turned and ran back to him. The grass of the pasture was soaked red around him. Now I was really bawling. I knelt down next to him as he slowly lifted his head, so I sat and cradled it in my lap. I stroked that curly steel-wool hair of his as his breath slowly grew faint. Then it stopped.

Little Garth was the first friend I lost. His death, my first encounter with mortality. It made things come into focus for me when I was very young. I learned that there are certain things in life that a person needs to stand up for. That there are battles that need to be fought, win or lose. No matter what the odds. And friendship and loyalty counts for something.

Later that week, El Toro broke the fence and got out onto the railroad tracks. I guess he figured he owned them too. The morning freight train came through doing about fifty and scattered him for a hundred yards down the tracks. When I saw his tail hanging on the railroad fence, I walked over and got my spinner back. I caught Old Lead Pencil on it later that afternoon.

MAY 58

~

Horsing a Potato Hook

I'm from a family of six kids. As in a lot of families back in the '60s, my mom ran the household and my dad ran the family. He did so with a dry wit and a firm hand, with an occasional foot in the ass when one of us needed discipline. Dad believed in a strong work ethic and instilled one in me at an early age.

I recall when I was about ten years old, my dad came in the house and said, "Son, how would you like to be a pilot?"

"Yeah! I'd love to be a pilot." I jumped at the idea.
"Good." he said. "I just dumped a load of firewood by the woodshed. Get your butt out there and pile-it."

He used this same principle in the summer when he'd have me piling hay bales. Those days haying were usually hotter than two rats screwing in a wool sock. I'd be in the back of the truck, sweating like the pig that knows he's dinner, when sooner or later my dad would gently set a bale on the tailgate of the truck and say, "Careful, Boy. This here's a tender one."

Since I was the "pile-it" on the truck, too, I'd learned that when my dad called a bale "tender," it was time to worry. It meant the bale was a large, hay-filled Slinky that I had to get into the barn without busting.

And I would have liked to run for the hills when one did break. The Old Man would start in.

"You broke a bale?! You must've yanked on the strings!" But even more likely, I'd hear, "You horsed it!"

Horsing it was one of his favorite expressions. Mostly because it was so darn versatile. You could horse just about anything. From a fish on the line to a lawn mower. I was once accused of horsing a potato hook. And in my Old Man's eyes, spearing a potato with your potato hook was right up there with busting a bale.

Of course, if he broke a bale, it was a different story.

Then he'd say, "That knotter on the baler must need greasing. A bale just broke on me." Like he was the victim of some great, grease-hoarding conspiracy cooked up by the baler. One of many forces arraigned against him to thwart his efforts to bale dry hay.

To the Old Man, having your hay rained on was an insult equivalent to somebody's pissing on your boots. He had a long-standing love-hate relationship seesawing back and forth with the Weatherman. Once, he was racing home from work to bale hay when a cop gave him the only speeding ticket he ever received. The predicted storm he was trying to beat never materialized. Hence, the hate part of the relationship.

And, when it came to digging potatoes, Dad could spear one himself and not bat an eye. In fact, according to him, it was an evolutionary aberration when he speared one.

"Must have been one that grew outside of the hill," he'd announce as he pulled the impaled mutant off the end of his hook. He'd stare disgustedly at it, as if it were a mongrel, renegade potato that deserved what it got by being different and not behaving like a good potato should.

It seemed as though it was always the first cold, nasty, raw, rainy weekend in the fall when passersby could find us kids out in the garden picking up the spuds. My dad would crack a verbal whip over us like we were a young chain gang filling bushel baskets. We put up twenty-five to thirty bushels. It wasn't a five-minute affair. We had to wash and sort them too.

The prelude to tater digging always moved over us kids like a black cloud. We would be sitting down at the supper table when the Old Man would make his pronouncement. "The Weatherman's calling for sleet and freezing rain on Saturday. But he lies so much I bet he has to get somebody else to call his dog. Sounds like a good day to dig them spuds out of the ground."

Six heads would bob up from supper plates with groans and stares of dread. He loved to torture us at the supper table. The highest form culminated in his chasing us around the table with a big dollop of horseradish on a spoon. We all hoped that he wouldn't shovel it into our mouths if he caught us. But we never knew for sure. This was his own cherished brand of amusement that he knew he could get away with. He was the head honcho. The Grand High Poo-bah. He reigned supreme within the family pecking order.

As his offspring, we felt it was our sworn duty to evade, elude, and otherwise circumvent this authority. Especially as we became teenagers. It was a goal we seldom reached.

Because trying to outsmart my Old Man was like trying to sneak sunrise past a rooster.

I was the youngest and always thought I could benefit by seeing how my older siblings fared in their persistent but usually fruitless attempts to outwit my father. It was the equivalent of watching game tapes of an opponent you'll face later in the season. My siblings would say that they had worn him down and made it easier for me. My reply to them is an emphatic screw you. I had it tougher. They'd sharpened his skills by repeated practice.

My only older brother was a shining example of what not to do. George was two years older than me and either lacked common sense or was just plain stupid. I once overheard my neighbor's dad talking about him. He said if stupid could fly, George would be a jet.

When he was about fifteen, George walked into the house one morning with a couple of his friends. They were coming in from a camp-out down back. They looked like they'd been sorting bobcats in a burning barn.

George told my mom that they'd been playing hide-and-seek and gotten into some berry bushes in the dark. We soon found out that they'd walked into town during the night to visit some girls. Too lazy to walk home, they'd decided to hop a train as it putted through town and past our place a mile or so down the line.

But they didn't foresee the engineer's opening the throttle up as soon as he'd cleared the village. That train was just a-steaming along about fifty when they had to bail off into the puckerbrush alongside the tracks. George admitted it was as painful as it sounded.

Thankfully, the fence that ran alongside the tracks had prevented them from landing in the river. Sort of like pinballs hitting the bumpers. They would've gotten away with it too, if a family friend hadn't seen them hanging off the train as he was waiting in his car at a crossing gate on his way home from the night shift. He called the Old Man. He said George had waved to him.

You would think being grounded for three weeks would have slowed George down a bit, but no. A week later he was caught with some of the same buddies on the roof of the new Essex High School that was under construction. This got him a week's suspension from the old high school.

It was during this suspension that he painted our house. My Mom made him start in the mornings painting the backside where nobody could see him. When school let out, she'd bring him around to the front.

Of course, the whole town already knew about George's suspension, but this strategy made Mom feel better. George was beyond shame.

"You missed a spot," I pointed out to him as I watched him painting.

"If I want any crap from you, I'll squeeze your head," George replied. His threat wasn't without substance. He would abuse me whenever the mood hit him, which was most of the time.

My cousin Donny and I once engaged him in battle, and I made the mistake of wearing a football helmet for protection. I soon found out why the NFL has penalties for face-mask infractions. George got hold of mine and swung me around in circles by my head while he laughed hysterically.

Donny saved me from a permanently stretched neck by sneaking up and clubbing George upside the head with a whiffle ball bat. I screwed that helmet off when George dropped me to pursue Donny.

A good kid will go only so far to circumvent his father's authority. But the distance is likely to lengthen when the hot-blooded romantic desires of a teenage boy are factored in. My quest to quench those desires led to the greatest deceptive exploit I ever attempted on the Old Man.

In the summer of '73 I'd turned sixteen and gotten my driver's license. The way I saw it, it wasn't just a license to drive, it was a license to park. With a girl. And I had one of those.

Martha Darling was prettier than a Jersey heifer in a clover patch. She hung a little too high on the limb for me though and was a terrible tease. She'd give me just a whiff of the stopper and then run off with the jug. So what I needed was a good secluded spot to ply my romantic skills to wear her defenses down. The driveway of our deer camp about twelve miles away was perfect. And for a while, things were great. I was happier than a woodchuck in soft dirt.

But then I got greedy. I thought as long as we were there, it sure would be nice to go inside the camp. There were beds inside. And it was that greed that let my little head start doing the thinking.

Because there was only one key to camp that I knew of. And it was in a place that no kid had ever gone before: the wallet of my Old Man. And that wallet, for all practical purposes, was fairly well glued to my Old Man's ass.

The challenge was daunting. My motives were substantial. My mission clear. I devised a plan.

Surveillance revealed that on most weekends, my parents would go out at least once. This would require the Old Man, as he so elegantly put it, to "shit, shave, shower, and shampoo." This performance always occurred in the basement bathroom. But he left his wallet on the bureau next to his bed upstairs.

Being a creature of habit and having been parboiled a few times, he would always shout, "GOING IN!" at the top of his lungs before he got under the shower head. This yell was to warn off any upstairs toilet-flushers and avoid being scalded like a pig again. On the chosen evening, this was also my secret battle cry. Because I was going in.

I slipped into my parents' bedroom like James Bond going for the microfilm. I stared at the wallet in front of me, and I hesitated for a moment. Almost like I thought it was rigged to go off. I memorized how it was facing, which side was down, and as I picked it up, I noticed my hands were shaking like a fifty-cent ladder. I took the coveted key out of his wallet and slid it into my pocket. I replaced the wallet back on the bureau, perfectly, and walked out. Now there was no turning back.

I hopped in the car, blasted up to the hardware store and had a key made. I jumped back in the car and blasted back home. And as I walked toward my parents' bedroom, I heard Dad's footsteps coming up the stairs. I was too late.

If he went up to camp before I could replace the key, my hopes of getting into camp—and my girlfriend's pants—were shot to hell. Because a week before, a game warden had seen my car parked at the camp and had called my dad with my license plate number. And I had lied my way out of it. I told him I was there berry picking with my girlfriend. I was picking berries all right! But if his camp key came up missing, he was smart enough to connect the dots.

So I pray to whatever gods I hope exist in this world watching out for horny teenagers, to come to my aid. And I took my time. I watched and waited. I didn't horse it. And the next weekend, I not only restored the key but also my faith in the power of prayer.

TURD GRADE

First grade was so much fun I got to thinking school was always going to be that way. My teacher, Miss Ivy, was so sweet and young that I felt as though a loving, older sister was teaching me. She praised us for completing even the simplest lessons. And even if I didn't get things done to perfection, she'd congratulate me for trying my best.

Second grade came along and with it a quite different, yet wonderful, teacher.

Mrs. Bigelow was an older, matronly woman who had kids of her own still in school. She understood how to get the best from her students by using kindness and sincerely caring for the individuals we were. And although she wouldn't tolerate disruptive behavior, she firmly used compassion and gentleness as the keys to opening our young minds.

And then came third grade. Or as we came to call it, turd grade. My third-grade classmates and I were incarcerated at the Little White Schoolhouse on the corner of Routes 15 and 128 in Essex Center. The rest of the first- through eighth-grade classes were located a couple of hundred yards farther down Route 128 at Hardstick Elementary. We were as good as on Alcatraz, cut off from the mainland.

And the High Warden of the penitentiary was my teacher, Mrs. Asbun. Or, as we came to call her, Mrs. Assburn. It was 1965, and corporal punishment was alive and thriving at the Little White Schoolhouse.

Ol' Assburn ran her classroom with strict authority. She made it clear that we were to sit up straight and pay attention. Toe the line, or pay the consequences.

Maybe she was so strict because she knew we'd been treated with kindness in our earlier schooling, and she thought we were soft slackers. Or maybe it was because we were getting older and exploring the disciplinary boundaries of the educational system and needed to be reined in. Then again, it might've been that she was just plain mean. Meaner than a stepped on cat. I vote for that assumption.

It soon became clear that she had many ways to dish out punishment for any distraction, disturbance, or the least little commotion. For instance, if you gave her any lip or spoke out of turn, she'd make you stick your tongue out and she'd clip a clothes pin on it. Her favorite form of penalty was the reliable stand-with-your-nose-in-the-corner routine.

Crude but effective, it served only to strengthen the resolve of some of the more rebellious students among our ranks. John Cady spent half of the year with his nose in one corner or another. His was a spirit that Ol' Assburn couldn't crush. A brain that she couldn't mold to following rules and directions.

Agitator, boatrocker, thorn-in-the side, John was the eight-year-old ringleader of the band of brothers loosely joined to pester and annoy Ol' Assburn during our year's sentence under her reign of terror.

Early in the year during art class we were all working diligently with our crayons as Ol' Assburn paced up and down between the rows of desks like a striker on a ship rowed by galley slaves. Scott Arnott raised his hand and said, "Anybody got a red crayon I can borrow?"

"I do," John Cady said, and tossed a red crayon across the room at Scott. Scott missed the catch and the crayon bounced off the globe beyond him with a nice ping.

Ol' Assburn walked over and picked up the crayon. She marched over to Cady's desk and grabbed him by the back of the neck like you'd pick up a hound-dog pup.

She escorted him to the front of the classroom and over to one side. We thought he was heading for the nose-in-the-corner drill for the rest of the day. We were mistaken.

She stopped a few feet from the wall and placed the crayon on the floor.

"Mr. Cady, you need to learn a better way to get a crayon across the room. Get down on your hands and knees, and roll it across."

John got down on his hands and knees. As he reached for the crayon with his bent index finger, as if he were going to shoot a marble, she said, "Not with your finger. With your nose."

Cady looked up at her in disbelief. "Get to it, Mr. Cady. Nobody throws crayons in my class."

John started nudging the red crayon across the old wood floor of the classroom with his beak. By the time he reached the other side, he had scraped his nose so much that it was bleeding. The first blood had been drawn. Of course, this meant war.

Gender provided little protection, the girls in our class learned. The day after I had received a tetanus shot, I was out at recess chasing girls around the playground. The unwritten statutes of the third grade boy/girl limited contact clause demanded this. I was like the dog that chases after a car: I wouldn't have known what to do with one if I'd caught it.

During a skirmish in the far corner of the playground, I briefly had Laura Barkcomb cornered. I impulsively grabbed at the ribbon tied in a bow on the back of her dress as she turned to escape. It was similar to a native warrior counting coup on his adversaries during battle. But I didn't realize that the ribbon was sewed on. The ribbon came off, but the act tore her dress.

Seeing too late the extent of the damage, I dropped the ribbon and sheepishly trotted off like a three-legged cow. Soon Ol' Assburn rang the handbell to bring us in. We all piled into the classroom and, as I sat down in my desk, Laura came up to me.

"How's that arm feeling?" she asked.

"Huh?" I replied. She was the prettiest girl in the class, and this lengthy conversation had me stymied. Maybe my smooth dress-ripping maneuver had endeared me to her?

"Which arm was it you got that shot in?" she coyly continued.

"My left one, right here" I said and pointed to the spot. Maybe she wanted to kiss it and make it better.

Wham! She drilled a knuckle sandwich with her bony little fist right into the spot where I'd gotten my tetanus shot. Woowee! I almost hit the ceiling, desk and all. Then I saw Ol' Assburn standing in the doorway. She'd seen the whole thing.

"Laura Barcomb!" she growled as she strode into the room. When she went by her front desk, she scooped up The Ruler. Not your ordinary foot-long measuring device, this one was a legend throughout the halls of Hardstick Elementary. Possibly even how the school got its name.

The Ruler was a good six inches longer and twice as thick and wide as normal rulers. It was carved from rock maple, and rumor had it that the marks on it weren't for measuring but recorded the number of students who'd had their hides tanned by it. Like the notches on a gunslinger's pistol.

It made a solid, hair-raising whacking noise as Ol' Assburn slapped it into the palm of her empty hand, advancing on the little girl standing next to my desk.

To her credit, Laura didn't squeal on me about the ribbon-tearing episode. Maybe she was too scared to talk. Maybe she was too scared to think. I know I sure was.

"Hold out your hand," Ol' Assburn said.

Laura stretched her tiny, trembling hand out in front of her. Ol' Assburn grabbed it by the fingertips and held it tight and still.

Three good solid cracks of The Ruler hit Laura's bare knuckles. I cringed as each one hit. But I didn't say a word. I couldn't say a word. I found it hard to even to breathe. I would've liked to have told Laura that it hurt me as much as it did her, but from the sound of her little gasps and the tears that rolled down her cheek, I knew it wasn't even close.

"How'd you like that, young lady? If anybody's going to get hit around here, I'll be the one doing it." The old biddy turned and stalked back to her desk.

When she plopped her ass down in her chair, she let out a shriek that could've been heard up at the main school building. A shriek greeted with internal glee by every oppressed third grader who had ever cowered under Ol' Assburn's sway.

Somebody had put a tack on her chair. Some brave, daring soldier of our rebel alliance had struck a small but effective blow into Assburn's backside.

When she grilled the class to try to find out the perpetrator, nobody spoke. She kept the whole class in for the afternoon recess with our heads down on our desks, but to no avail. There were no traitors. If anybody knew anything, they kept it to themselves.

On the bus ride home that day, I got to studying on who could've planted the tack on Ol' Assburn's chair. Who'd had the opportunity? Who'd had the guts to carry out such a dangerous mission?

Art Babcock, a kid from up on Lost Nation, had been assigned to clean erasers during recess. No, now that I thought about it, he had volunteered for the job. Kind of a teacher's pet sort of thing to do. Or was it a ploy to draw the hound off the scent?

I turned in my seat on the bus and looked at him where he sat a couple of rows back. I looked at him and raised my eyebrows, and smiled. He gave me just the slightest of nods and smiled back.

The next morning when he got on the bus, I offered him the seat beside me. We sat together from then on. All the way through eighth grade until we went to high school and we no longer rode the bus.

The tides of battle ebbed back and forth. At one point, Ol' Assburn called in the big guns. The school principal, Mr. Willphear, came down to the Little White Schoolhouse and gave us a talking-to.

Mr. Willphear was well over six feet tall with a Marine haircut and beak-like nose. He was known to grab any old kid he felt like by the scruff of the neck and drag his carcass off to his office to drub him at his leisure. Ol' Assburn asking him to visit was like calling in an aircraft carrier to the Persian Gulf in a show of strength.

Mr. Willphear appeared after one of Ol' Assburns's car doors was left slightly ajar. Just enough to turn the dome light on and kill the battery. It would take a mechanic's son to come up with something like that. I did what I could.

Headquarters for the Resistance was the boys' bathroom located in the dungeon-like basement of the old school. The stairway went down for about eight steps to a small landing, then turned ninety degrees to the right and descended another three steps. Ol' Assburn had never invaded this sanctuary, and we'd been lulled into a false sense of security.

To the right side of the small room was a toilet stall. To the left side was a small sink. Straight ahead, across from the bottom of those last three stairs and about six feet away was a long trough urinal that could accommodate three or four guys' whizzings at once.

There came a day late in the school year when a group of us guys were down in the bathroom together for a little R & R. John Cady came up with a brilliant sort of challenge: Which one of us, he wondered, could pee the farthest?

Ray Porter took the first go at it. His shot made it from where he started in front of the trough to the bottom of the stairs as he stepped backward while firing away. Respectable, but we thought we had stronger contestants among us. Hub Roby squeezed out a stream from a perch on the second stair that hit the trough perfectly, probably could have gone farther.

We were all laughing and squealing as eight-year-old boys tend to when having fun. And as I got up on the second step and started blasting away, I knew I could do better and backed up onto the third step. Still going strong and adjusting for Kentucky windage, I took another step up onto the little landing and nailed the trough dead center to the cheers of my fellow classmates.

Suddenly, a dark shadow loomed over me. Ol' Assburn grabbed me by the scruff of the neck. Trying to shut down the waterworks when they're going full blast isn't an easy task. Doing so and trying to zip up while being dragged up a flight of stairs is even tougher.

Unfortunately, I caught the frank and beans in the zipper for just a brief second, enough to make me yelp like a stung puppy. I managed to get things freed up and tucked away before Ol' Assburn dragged me bodily into the classroom.

She stood me in the corner with my nose firmly planted in it. She leaned down and I could smell her rank, cigarette and coffee-tainted breath.

"You so much as move your head one inch to one side or the other, and I'll paste you one you'll never forget," she whispered in my ear.

I don't know how long I stood there in the corner. Lord knows I couldn't see the clock. I do know it was all the way though recess and most of English class.

I sure did learn my lesson that day. One I could've applied to the whole year. Hell, for my whole life. When it comes to a pissing contest, there really aren't any winners.

~

SINGLED OUT

I got a bow and arrow when I was six. A Daisy BB gun when I turned seven. I had a pocketknife and a hatchet from then on, too. I made slingshots and spears. When you think about it, you really need a knife and a hatchet to make a good slingshot and a decent spear. Heck, making them is half the fun.

When I was twelve, I would get my first real firearm. At least that was what I believed from age ten on. My parents had let my older brother, George, get a gun when he turned twelve, so I figured I was entitled to one at that age, too. After all, we counted out M&Ms in our family to keep things equal. Even their colors. I didn't see where guns would be any different. A precedent had been set.

I wouldn't have trusted George with a sharp stick. I regarded my older brother as a prime example of God's carelessness. So when he received a twenty-gauge shotgun when he hit twelve, I knew my parents had set the bar pretty low.

Still, the Old Man wasn't going to make it easy for me. I learned early that most privileges in life have strings attached. Rules that must be obeyed. Rules that guide us to do things responsibly. Over the years I've come to realize that my marksmanship skills largely result from my dad's demanding high standards from his kids. As I look back, I realize the guns I learned on had certain limitations. And I believe my Old Man chose them on purpose. Made me a crack shot. I can still shoot the stink off a skunk at fifty paces.

I'd been shooting guns under my father's guidance since I was five. He had a single shot .410 gauge shotgun: an old Model 1929 Springfield that he used for all his rabbit-hunting. He had sawed the barrel off a couple of inches so it spread the little pattern of birdshot from its tiny shell quite wide.

In the world of hair triggers, this one was hairier than most. All you had to do was breathe lightly on it and she'd let go. But it was a good gun to learn on. You didn't get near the trigger until you were ready to shoot. There was little recoil to speak of. The scatter of shot was such that you rarely completely missed what you were aiming at. That gun built confidence in a young boy.

I recall trailing along behind my dad in the bright fall woods around our camp one day when I was six or seven. We had our two beagles, Buster and Buddy, a father and son combo. My dad stopped and said, "Watch Buster. The old boy's onto something." I could see the white tip of the dog's tail whipping back and forth a mile a minute as he worked into some briers next to a clump of thorn apple.

Wings suddenly exploded as a partridge rocketed out of the brush a few feet ahead of the hound. It dodged and twisted through the crisp fall air like a wobbly thrown football. My dad snapped the little .410 to his shoulder as he thumbed back the hammer. There was a sharp report as he swung on the bird, then a puff of feathers and a burst of red maple leaves. The partridge tumbled through the air, landing in a thick patch of ferns thirty yards away.

The ferns came alive all around the spot where it had fallen, and then a line of them swayed towards us as Buster emerged with the bird in his mouth. The Old Man reached down and took it from him, and patted him on the head.

"Good boy," he said as he broke open the little gun. It shot the spent cardboard cartridge over his right shoulder with a neat click and a pop.

"Ca'tridges for pa'tridges," he grinned and winked at me, and fished a fresh cartridge from his coat pocket.

I picked up the spent shell and brought it up to my nose, smelling the acrid odor of the freshly burned powder. That smell seared itself into my cranium. Always a reminder of fall days and my dad.

When I smell that aroma, I drift back, seeing the delicate mottled markings on the plump little bird. My Old Man knelt down and showed me the tiny topknot on its head. He told me that its real name was ruffed grouse. He fanned out its black-striped tail feathers.

"See this wide black band on his feathers and how complete it is all the way across?" he said. "That tells you most likely it's a cock bird, a male. A hen's color will usually fade slightly in the middle." He pointed out the feathered toes that act like fuzzy snowshoes. Then he tucked the bird into his game pouch, stood up, and called out to the dogs.

"Hunt 'em up, boys! Let's find a rabbit! Hunt 'em up!"

As we continued on our way, I couldn't help but think that partridge had to be the coolest bird in the whole dang forest. I dreamed of the day that I might have a shot at one with a gun of my own.

Even though I didn't have my own gun, I still got quite a bit of trigger time to learn about safety and hone my marksmanship. The Old Man allowed me to shoot his Winchester .22-caliber pump action rifle at targets and cans when we went to camp. We hardly ever shot the rifle at home. He made it clear that launching a piece of hot lead that can travel over a mile was a responsibility not to be taken lightly. The area around our home had too many things a stray bullet or ricochet could hit. The Old Man made it a hard-and-fast rule that a shooter must know not only what and where his target is but also what lies beyond it.

There weren't the hunter safety courses that are mandatory to get your hunting license these days. But our training on handling guns was second to none. And it was no idle threat when the Old Man said he would confiscate our weapons if we committed a safety transgression. And we might get a cuff aside the head for good measure.

On my twelfth birthday in August of 1969 I was high on anticipation when I received my mother's Stevens .410-bolt-action shotgun. That's when it dawned on me that the Old Man wasn't going to make it easy for me to get my first partridge.

That Stevens was a heavy gun for a scrawny kid like me. When I first hefted it, it seemed heavier than a dead preacher. But I lugged it everywhere I went and it toughened me up.

The barrel had a full choke. A full choke means that the shot pattern is kept as tight as possible for as far as possible. It was just the opposite of my Old Man's Springfield. To hit any-thing, you had to be dead on target. The pattern didn't spread out much until it got out beyond thirty yards or so. A rabbit with a dog on its trail is bouncing through thickets where you can scarcely see thirty yards away.

Partridge hunting during my first couple weeks with this gun was a tough row to hoe. The birds like to let you just about step on them before they flush. By the time they got out where my pattern opened up, the brush was too thick for a clear shot.

But that gun made me a good shot. Eventually. Even better, it made me a good hunter. It made me learn patience. And patience makes all the difference when traveling through the woods. Traveling through life.

I killed my first partridge as it sat on the ground under a small spruce tree. I didn't think it was absolutely fair to shoot him on the ground with my shotgun, but I was desperate to bring home a bird. My mom cooked it for supper that night, and I was happier than a skinny flea on a fat dog. I had broken the ice in the partridge-hunting world.

I learned a lot about bird hunting that fall. For one, I took note of what the birds were eating and where I was flushing them. I found that later in the season, when the autumn leaves had fallen and the woods opened up, I could wait a bit and take my shot a bit farther out where my pattern was wider.

I never shot another partridge that wasn't on the wing with a shotgun. Killing a sitting bird with a rifle, well, that was a different matter. If you could hit one with that one bullet that a rifle affords, it was considered fair chase hunting.

I'd gotten my own .22-caliber rifle on my fourteenth birth-day. The Old Man had taken me to Gaynes Shopper's World and told me that I could pick one out. All my friends had bolt-actions or pumps, and one had a semi-automatic. I asked my dad which one he would pick. He pointed down to the end of the rack at a little Ithaca. It looked like a lever-action, but it was actually a falling-block single-shot. When the hunter pulls the lever downward on this kind of gun, the block in front of the chamber slides down. The hunter puts a shell in it, pulls the lever back up, then pulls the hammer back, and it fires. A lengthy process for a 14-year-old kid.

"That one there would do the job," Dad said. "It will save you on ammo and make you think about every shot you take, so you make it a good one." I was eyeballing a semi- automatic Marlin that had a much larger shot capacity. I figured I could load it on a Sunday and shoot all week. It was twice the money of the Ithaca.

"I need a new pair of work gloves," the Old Man said. "My old ones are played out. Why don't you study on it and I'll be back in a little while?" and he wandered off to get his gloves.

An old clerk came up to me from behind the counter as I stood there gazing at that Marlin.

"Hi, young feller. I couldn't help but overhear you and your dad talking. That Marlin sure is a smart-shooting rifle. I'd be glad to sell it to you. But ya know, I've hunted all my life. Everything from birds to bears. One thing I've come to learn is, most generally, all you ever get at a critter is one shot, and you best make it count. It seems to me the choice between those two guns is the same as whether you want to be a hunter, or a shooter."

I knew the old clerk was right. I also felt deeply obligated to do what the Old Man wanted. The fact was we weren't flush with money. My two older sisters were in college, and I knew the family was strapped for funds. Maybe that was why I'd gotten my mom's Stevens on my twelfth birthday instead of a new gun.

When Dad came back, I told him of my choice and the smile on his face was worth the ribbing I knew I would take from my friends. What kind of an idiot would choose a puny single-shot when he had the pick of the litter? What sort of fourteen-year-old boy would choose a lesser birthday gift and harassment from his friends? Deep down, where words aren't spoken, I knew what kind.

My dad threw in 500 rounds of .22 ammo to sweeten the deal. As we were driving home, I cradled the gun like a newborn babe. I got to looking at the receipt from the store. Scrawled in the old clerk's handwriting were the words, "10% hunter discount."

CASTING CALL

In my earliest memories of fishing I'm holding a long bamboo pole with a length of line on it. A bobber and a hook are on the line, and I swing it out into the water.

It was such a simple way to fish. Even a five year old could catch something. When the red-and-white bobber started jumping up and down, it was magical. The tug on the pole was a jolt of energy that transferred directly to the joy bone tucked somewhere inside my five-year-old body. For me, pulling that first perch from the water was like pulling a rabbit out of a hat. And I wanted to do it again and again.

The Winooski River ran behind my house. To get to the river, I had to cross a couple of our pastures as well as the railroad tracks. It wasn't like I could fall out my bedroom window and land in it. But that was how my mother perceived the river. She was terrified I would drown if I got within a stone's throw of it.

My brother, George, was a good swimmer. But fishing didn't have the fascination for him it did for me. He could take it or leave it. The biggest reason we didn't fish much together, though, was that we irritated the hell out of each other. But even then I was a firm believer that you have to keep swinging at the pitches you're thrown, so I kept begging George to take me fishing down back. The results were lackluster. As on one summer day at lunchtime.

"Come on George. It'll be fun! I'll clean any fish we keep, and you can have your pick at supper." I figured I'd try the carrot-on-a-stick method. George was an eater. He was currently chowing down a peanut butter and jelly sandwich as if he were stuffing a musket.

"I've already got the worms dug. They'll go bad if we don't use them. You don't want the death of innocent worms on your conscience, do you?" Maybe feeling guilty would make him go fishing.

"I see you don't mind sticking them on a hook and feeding them to a fish," he pointed out.

"That's for a good cause," I said. "We all have to make sacrifices. Yours could be to take me fishing."

"You're like a fly that keeps landing on the same spot, ain't ya? Irritating as hell and needs to be slapped. Why don't you quit pestering me and just learn how to swim? Stop being such a scaredy-pants."

George got up to raid the cookie jar. I could see this conversation wasn't going anywhere. Maybe I ought to leave. George could get ornery. I eased towards the screen door of the kitchen.

"It's a lot easier for you to swim than it is for me," I said.

"Why's that?" he asked.

I opened the screen door and shut it behind me, turned, and said through the screen, slowly and clearly, "Turds float."

Having flipped the lock on the screen door as I went through, I safely, but quickly, left the premises. The screen door might not slow George down much.

Luckily for me, there were other anglers in the neighborhood I could fish with and who swam well. I hooked up with them whenever I could, and I was able to wet a line fairly often.

This same summer I started to make friends with Kirk Perkins. Kirk lived about a mile down Route 117 on his family's dairy farm. The Winooski River was right across the road from their farmhouse, and Kirk's dad bought him a brand new twelve-foot flat-bottom john boat from Sears.

Kirk was an only child and got 'most everything he asked for. He always had the newest, hottest toys on the market. But I hardly ever saw him play with them, at least not when I was there. He would show them to me, say how he didn't feel like playing with them, and then suggest we do something else that he did feel like doing.

And that worked out fine if he wanted to take his boat out fishing. We'd start the excursion by getting some live bait. Alder Brook crossed the road a couple hundred yards past Kirk's house before it spilled into the Winooski. He had a minnow trap in a pool next to the road. We'd pull it up by the baler twine attached to it and see what we had. If there wasn't anything in it, Kirk had a minnow net that we could use in the eight-foot-wide brook.

We'd take the three-foot-tall net and stretch it between us on the two stakes it was attached to and slowly work it upstream. We would get lots of candidates for the bait bucket.

Shiners, dace, and sucker minnows. Maybe a few frogs or tadpoles. Small crayfish made some of the best bait for catching bass. It was just as much fun catching the bait as it was catching the fish.

Once we had a sufficient amount of bait we'd head for the Winooski. We used a twelve-year-old Armstrong propulsion system to navigate the boat. Kirk rowed.

After a couple of summers, we knew every pool, riffle, and rock within a half mile upstream or downstream of Kirk's farm. All the most likely spots that would hold a fish and where to cast to catch them.

We would get pretty focused on making a good cast. Looking intently at the spot we'd want to cast to, we sometimes forgot that the backcast behind us needed some consideration too. A twelve-foot boat doesn't allow a lot of room for casting. Kirk took my hat right off my head with his backcast once. Gave me quite a start.

Not nearly as bad as the one that I gave Kirk one day, though. He was fishing wearing a tank top. When a nice bass made a rise off to the port side, I swung around and whipped my rod at it with a short wrist cast and buried my orange Abu Spinner into Kirk's left- side armpit hair. He hit a high note better than a soprano in a boys' choir.

Kirk got the last laugh, though. On another outing, while tying a hook to my line, I held it between my teeth and gave it a quick little tug to tighten the knot. The hook slipped loose and I buried the barbed hook into my lower lip. And that's where it stayed for a while. The fish were really biting good. Kirk offered to have a go at that hook with a pair of rusty needle- nose pliers he had in his tackle box. "If you let me come over and give it a shot, I bet I can worry it out of there for ya," he said.

"Yeah, and if your aunt had nuts she'd be your uncle. You just stay put right where you are. The only thing you're worrying with those pliers is me. Put them things away."

When I finally pedaled my bike home, my Mom was working in the kitchen. As I walked in, she didn't hardly look up at me.

"You're back from fishing. Did you catch anything?" she asked.

I pulled on the hook lightly, and it pulled my lip out as she finally took a good gander at her youngest child.

"Just one," I answered. "A big sucker."

We ended up going to the doctor's office. Doc Patterson gave me a shot of Novocain in my lip and then shoved the hook through it the rest of the way and snipped the barb off and backed it out. He said it wasn't the first time he'd performed the procedure, and as long as there were kids fishing, it probably wouldn't be the last.

Out of Range

Opening day of trout season in Vermont arrives on the second Saturday of April. Spring can sometimes take a little longer to get here. I've tromped through snow, hiking in to get to some beaver ponds on opening day, only to arrive and have them still iced over except for a spot or two where the water comes in or a spring creates a hole in the ice.

Not to be denied, I've cast my worm beyond the hole, dragged it back until it fell into the water. And sure as a goose goes barefoot, I'd feel a tug on my line and drag a nice brookie up out of the water and skid it, flipping and flopping, across the ice to me. The legal size was six inches or longer and twelve fish for a daily limit. A six incher was a keeper. An eight incher was a nice one. Any fish over ten inches was a real eye popper.

I don't know of any other freshwater fish that is prettier than a native Vermont brook trout. Their bright orange bellies and yellow, red, and blue dots against the dark mottled background are set off by the black and white striping on their fins. A marvel to look at.

No scaling is required before frying them. And nothing in this world tastes better than freshly caught brookies rolled in a bit of flour and cornmeal and fried in some real creamery butter.

One spring, while fishing the string of beaver ponds below our camp, I ran onto a local kid from up the road. His name was Harvey Mallard, and he was the son of Windy Mallard, a man well-known in the region for his woodsmanship, both legal and otherwise. Harvey and I hit it off. He was a year younger than I, but we never noticed the difference.

During the course of one summer, we fished a lot of the local fishing spots together that were within easy walking distance. The pickings were starting to get a bit thin as the summer wore on, when Harvey suggested we try someplace else.

"Why don't you bring your bike up next weekend, and I'll take you to one of my secret spots," he said. "It takes about forty-five minutes to bike in to this chain of beaver ponds, but it's worth the ride. The trout are long as your arm."

"You're funning me. Ain't no brook trout that long," I said.

"Well, maybe not that long, but you wait and see. And if we have the time to hit a gorge I know of on Lee River, we can latch onto some rainbows or browns."

"Lee River?" I said. "Isn't that over on the Firing Range?"

"Yeah, so what?" Harvey replied. "You ain't scared to go over there, are you? My dad goes over there all the time. It has some of the best hunting and fishing around."

"No, I ain't scared. How big did you say those trout were?" I could picture beaver ponds teeming with foot-long brookies leaping to get into my creel.

Now, my dad never told me not to go on the Range. This was the Ethan Allen Firing Range where G.E. tested its Gatling guns that could shoot more than 200 bullets per second. He probably figured that I wasn't so stupid he needed to tell me. This wasn't the first time he'd underestimated my aptitude on this subject.

The Range is an 11,000-acre piece of property also used as a training ground for Army soldiers and National Guardsmen, both Army and Air Force, and strictly off limits to civilians. Its roads and boundaries are guarded by the Range Patrol, and they don't take kindly to trespassers. I figured it'd be best if I just didn't mention to my Old Man exactly where Harvey and I were planning on fishing.

"What do you need your bike for?" my dad asked, as I put it into the back of his pickup before we left for camp the next Saturday morning.

"Oh, Harvey and I are going to use our bikes to go fish Mill Brook. We're getting tired of walking down there," I answered.

Mill Brook was on the border of the Range and therefore in the direction we needed to go.

Harvey and I stopped and untied our poles from the frames of our bikes and fished the swimming hole by the bridge on Mill Brook on our way to the Range. Now if my dad asked where I'd fished, I could answer in all honesty, as a good son should.

Harvey and I didn't even get a nibble at the swimming hole, so we rode up to one of the many unguarded gates located at various points around the Range. This one was on the road to the old West Bolton Cemetery.

There was a well-worn path that led around the gate and back onto the road beyond it. From there on, I was doing the best I could to keep up with Harvey. That little beggar could pedal. There were woods along either side of the road for the most part with an occasional abandoned farmstead clearing. At the top of a particularly long hill, we stopped to catch our breath.

"How much farther?" I panted.

"Not much."

"You hear something? Shit! Get off the road!" Harvey grabbed his bike and headed off the road into the scrub brush with me tight on his heels. About twenty feet off the road there was an old stonewall, and we threw our bikes and ourselves over it and flattened out as a Jeep with three soldiers in it drove by, the words Range Patrol clearly stenciled on the side of it. Then six humongous tanks went pounding by. The black clouds of their exhaust drifted over us and stung our eyes.

"Holy shit! That was close!" I said as the size of the trout shrunk a good four inches in my head.

"Ah, that was nothing," said Harvey. "I outfox them all the time. Come on. We're almost there."

We got back on the road, my head swiveling back and forth like an owl's as I tried to watch both ways. We went about a quarter of a mile down the road, and Harvey took a left-hand turn onto a lightly used two-tracked trail. As we pedaled along, I noticed a hillside off to the right up ahead of us. It looked strange compared to the heavy green foliage of the nearby hills.

We got closer to it, and the woods opened up and we were in a large field. On the far side of the field, down off to the left, lay a series of beautiful beaver ponds bounded by a wooded ridge on the far side. I think I started to drool.

The hill I had seen was now off to the right, beyond the

distant, higher end of the meadow. I turned and looked in that direction and all drooling ceased. Every tree in a swath 300 yards wide and all the way to the top of the rise was mowed off. Trees lay in tangled heaps like pick-up sticks. Trees ten to twenty inches in diameter, pruned off in ragged splitters a few feet off the ground.

"What the hell happened there?" I asked

"Vulcan guns, Minnie guns. You know, Gatling guns," Harvey said. "We're in the Cone of Fire. This is damn close to the Impact Zone."

"Cone of Fire!? Impact Zone!? Are you serious?"

"Oh, don't get your panties in a bunch. They don't shoot much on weekends," Harvey answered as we untied our poles and stashed our bikes out of sight.

"Let's try that first pond right there. We'll ease out on the lower side of the dam then climb up just enough to cast over it."

We walked over to the dam and worked our way into position about thirty feet apart. I took a worm out of my worm box and baited up. I cast about twenty feet out into the pond and before my worm could hit the bottom, I had a trout on.

"Don't keep anything under eight inches unless it swallows the hook." Harvey reeled in a fat ten-incher.

We yanked in three nice brookies each. I nailed one a good foot long.

We left the first pond and moved down for a repeat performance at the second one. This time I caught four trout, all nine- and ten-inch beauties, while Harvey snagged five. One was a bit bigger than the monster I'd caught.

As we left the second pond, Harvey said, "Let's finish off our limit at Lee River. It's not far from here. We can catch some nice browns and rainbows."

I reluctantly agreed, only because if he was willing to leave this spot for someplace else, it had to be good. We walked up to our bikes and were tying our rods onto them when Harvey's head shot up like Radar's on M*A*S*H.

"Choppers!" he yelled. "Get out of sight!"

We grabbed our bikes and pushed them, running into the woods on the trail we'd come in on as the pounding of rotor blades grew louder. We could still see out into the field, but the dense canopy of the trees gave us the illusion of safety. The illusion disappeared when two helicopters, one a few hundred yards behind the other, flew over the field only a couple hundred feet off the ground.

As the first one went over the ponds we were just fishing, the door gunner gave about a three-second burst with his Minnie Gun and strafed the ponds. The chopper rose up a bit and turned to its right and let go a five-second burst into the shredded hillside above and to the right. The hillside exploded with dirt and debris. The second one followed the same routine.

The noise was ear-shattering. My eyes bugged out like a stepped-on toad's, "Christ Almighty, Mallard! I thought you said they didn't shoot on weekends!?"

"I said they didn't shoot much!" he replied. "Apparently they've got something going on. We've got to get the hell out of here!"

He didn't have to talk me into it. We saddled up and lit out like we had some place to go and it was on fire. We had to bail off our bikes and hide roadside three more times when groups of tanks went by. It seemed like they were everywhere. Thankfully, a convoy of tanks can't sneak up on a person because your bike starts shaking like a dog passing a pine cone along with a loud growling sound like a wounded bear.

The last half-mile of road leading to the gate was sparsely wooded and open entirely in spots. We were losing steam but found our second wind when a helicopter came over a ridge and spotted us. It bore right down on top of us, just above the treetops. We could feel the wind from the blades. Harvey looked up at the chopper pilot and flipped him the bird.

"Great!" I thought. "Let's really piss them off."

"Keep going!" yelled Harvey. "They're trying to pin us down so they can radio the Range Patrol to come catch us!"

That was just the enticement I needed. It was slightly downhill to the gate. The chopper hovered straight above us as we hurled ourselves down the road and around the gate like we were in the Tour de France, vying for the yellow jersey. We were almost out of sight of the gate when we stopped to catch our breath and look back. The Range Patrol Jeep pulled up to the gate. And then it turned around and left.

We casually straddled our bikes and started pedaling along at a leisurely pace.

"Well, we didn't catch our limit," Harvey sighed.

"We didn't get to fish Lee River either," I remarked. "Big browns and rainbows in there, huh?"

"Brookies, too. Longer'n Dad's pecker," Harvey replied as we rounded a bend on the sun-shaded road. We coasted to a stop on the bridge over Mill Brook and watched a few kids playing in the cool, clear water of the swimming hole.

"So, what do you think of my taking you over on the Range?" Mallard asked.

"Tanks, Harvey. Tanks a lot."

~

HOUND DOGS ON THE HUNT

The gods of the hills are not the gods of the valleys. So said Ethan Allen, who was one of Vermont's favorite sons and was most likely swilling rum at the time. I was never quite sure what the old hero meant by that phrase. But I'm beginning to, because I live in those hills. And over the years, I've noticed that the winters sure are different from what they are down in the valleys. I'm starting to think God invented winter in the hills of Vermont just in case forever ain't quite long enough. Sometimes, it feels like we have just two seasons: this winter and the next.

When I was a kid, winter was something I looked forward to. We would have snowball fights and build snow forts and jumps for our saucers, sleds, and skis. We'd go ice skating and ice fishing and snowmobiling.

One of the most enjoyable outings for us during the winter months was going rabbit hunting. Snowshoe rabbit hunting. They're actually varying hares because their coats turn white in the winter. And if you ever saw the size of their hind feet, you'd know why they're called snowshoe rabbits. Also, the imprint left in the snow where their hind feet reach in front of their narrow front feet as they run is a paddle-shaped track that resembles one made by a small snowshoe.

We always had a couple of beagles for rabbit hunting. To be accurate, we used them for rabbit chasing. From what I could surmise, the main purpose of rabbit hunting was to see how good our dogs were compared to the dogs owned by the friends and associates we hunted with.

There's something intriguing and exciting about entering a snow- covered swamp to hunt snowshoe hares. First, we'd try to start the dogs on a track. Once we accomplished that, we'd position ourselves to get a glimpse of the rabbit as the dogs chased it. Snowshoe rabbits tend to run in a large circle when dogs are pursuing them. They rarely go into a hole in the ground as cottontail rabbits do. This habit allowed us to make educated guesses as to where we might be able to rendezvous with the rabbit.

Shooting the rabbits was not all that high on our agenda. In fact, sometimes we frowned upon it. Especially if we felt we were overtaxing the population of snowshoe rabbits in some of our favorite swamps we hunted in. I'm pretty sure we were chasing the same rabbits from one weekend to the next. I'd sometimes imagine what the rabbits might be saying to each other.

"Damn it, Fred, here they come again! I can't remember whose turn it is. You want evens or odds? Evens? One, two, three, shoot! Five! Damn! I'd almost rather they'd just blast me as run me to death!" And the chase was on.

Sometimes we had to shoot a rabbit in order to catch the dogs and end the hunt. The most dedicated dogs were hard to call off the track. It could be quite frustrating trying to catch those little hounds. Like trying to nail Jello to a tree.

"Here he comes! Grab him!" the Old Man would yell at me as the barking came closer and closer on the track. The little dog would squirt around me on top of the crust of snow that I was sinking into past my knees.

"Why the hell didn't you grab him?!" Dad would say with a grin.

You could stand right in the tracks that the rabbit had made and still miss catching the determined little bugger. Those beagles would see you coming and go into evasive maneuvers to stay on the track. Sometimes they even went right between my legs.

The best time of the hunt would be at noon when we'd all gather somewhere in the swamp for lunch and start a rip-roaring blaze. Thermoses of hot chocolate or coffee or maybe some soup would be broken out of knapsacks. Everybody would cut a forked stick to lay their sandwiches on to toast them over the fire. Half the time they would be charcoaled on the outside and frozen on the inside, but they still tasted better than if they'd been grilled on the stove at home. We'd sit and talk of past hunts and listen to the sweet music of the dogs howling through the snow as a rabbit led them in circles around us.

Many times we had to leave a dog or two overnight because we couldn't get them off a hare's track. We'd leave a vehicle if we could, removing the dome light and propping a door open. Especially when it was brutally cold. We'd put an old jacket or dog blanket on the seat so the scent would be familiar to the lost hound. Or leave it right on the ground if we couldn't leave a rig.

The next day we'd go back and retrieve the worn-out pooch. If it had run all night, the inside edges of its ears would be all bloody from going through the brush. Sometimes the pads on its feet were bloody as well. Those beagles just loved to hunt and didn't know when to quit.

Once, our dog Buster was lost for five days in a snowstorm. I was worried to the point of tears. "Don't you fret none about old Buster," Dad said, "he can take care of himself. I'll bet you pigs to polecats that we'll find him safe and sound sooner or later."

But those words were little comfort to a young kid lying in bed at night, listening to the wind howling a blizzard outside. Images of Buster alone, freezing, hurt, and starving were all that I could think of.

We finally found him shacked up in a hardscrabble homestead about three miles away from where we had lost him. A kid had found him and taken him in. Had him sleeping right in his bed with him. All the hair had frozen off Buster's tail. The Old Man started calling him our rat terrier.

There was one rabbit-running expedition when the Old Man went with Mutt Summers and Floogee Lackalade in Mutt's old Buick station wagon. They had the dogs in the far back, and one of them messed in the back while on route. The smell was so bad, they were hanging their heads out the windows instead of the dogs. Mutt pulled over and cleaned it up the best he could, and they kept going.

When they arrived at the hunting spot, Floogee jumped out, grabbed his coat and gun out of the back, and ran into the woods. So did the Old Man. This was standard procedure if you valued your life, firearm safety not being one of Mutt's strong suits. He never owned a vehicle that didn't have at least one or two bullet holes in the roof or floor boards. An hour or so later, Mutt and Floogee met up in the woods.

"Boy, that dog crap sure as hell stunk," Floogee said. "Well at least you didn't have to clean it up," said Mutt.

"Maybe so," said Floogee, "but I just can't get over how bad it was. I swear I can still smell it."

"I can see why," Mutt said. "If you turn your head to the right, you'll stick your nose in it. There's a big gob of it smeared on your coat collar." Floogee's jacket had been in the back with the dogs.

Those three argued for years about whose dog was the offender. Floogee swore our dog, Buster, was guilty, but the Old Man insisted Buster was of too high of breed stock to perform such a low act. He accused Floogee's dog, Bo-Bo. Neither dog would confess.

During his childhood, my dad had known many good dogs. His mother raised a strain of Collie-Shepherd cow dogs that fetched top dollar during the Depression. Dad liked to tell tales about his dog Ted. He swore Ted could just about talk. Or at least understand every word people said.

To prove his point, he recalled a day when his family had just sat down to supper one summer evening when his dad looked out the window and said, 'That fence-busting white heifer is out again.' Ted got up off the floor, nudged open the screen door, and went out and put her back in the pasture right through the hole she had gotten out of. When he was finished, he came in and lay down right back where he was to begin with. His dad looked at him and said, 'What took you so long?'

And it didn't matter if anybody was around or not, Ted would gather the cows for milking. Whether it was for first milking in the morning or the later afternoon one. If the family was gone or out in the fields, when they got back, all the cows would be nosed up to the barn door. Old Ted would be close by, lying in the shade. If one of the cows started to wander off, all he had to do was stand up and give a little "Woof!" The cow would head back to the barn. She knew it was no use to disagree with Ted.

Dad used to say to me, "Boy, you ain't dumber than Old Ted, but you ain't beating him by much either." It was probably as close to a compliment as I ever got.

But even the best dogs can have their faults, and Ted had two. He couldn't abide porcupines. He got stuck with quills many times. It would take a couple people to hold him down. One would use a two-pronged pitchfork and pin him to the ground just behind his head. The other would almost have to lie on top of him.

Dad's mother would use a pair of pliers and pull the quills out of him. It got so if she picked up a pair of scissors or anything else that resembled pliers, Old Ted would start growling and head for the woods.

Ted's other weakness was chasing deer. He just couldn't pass it up, and it was his downfall. He was about ten years old when he chased one out onto river ice, and they both broke through and drowned.

When I got into my teenage years, I was invited on some fox hunts with my best friend, Art. His grandfather, Gardner, was a dyed-in-the wool fox hunter and had a number of championship fox hounds over the years. One hunt I went on was enlightening.

"Gramps," said Art as we were getting ready, packing things into Gramps' old truck. "Don't you think we should leave Suzy home today? I think she's coming into heat."

"Nonsense," said Gramps, "she'd be heartbroken if we left her home."

Later in the hunt, we were sitting around a blazing fire in the snowy swamp and listening to the musical sounds of the dogs running. Gramps, who was a bit hard of hearing, turned to his grandson and asked him, "How they running, Boy?"

Art listened a bit and said, "Well, it sounds likes Suzy's right out front. And Old Jasper is a close second, and Rip is right behind him. I think the fox is running fourth."

And so I learned how the powers of sexual persuasion can turn even the best-behaved of boys into horny hound dogs. An enlightening hunt indeed.

THE TA-TA WEENIE CLUB

Lute Bouchard was a neighborhood kid who lived across the road from us. He was four years older than me, and a dominating figure in my childhood. He had a younger brother two years older than me whose nickname was Twitch. You could say Twitch was a bit high-strung.

If you met his mother, Florence, you'd know how he got that way. Florence's nickname was Flo. My dad said it was because she talked a steady stream. I never heard her husband, Urban, speak more than a few words in all the years I knew them. She wore the pants in the family. And judging by her disposition, I think they were chaffing her somewhere.

It's been said that genius has its limitations, whereas stupid can go full throttle. This pretty much explains Lute. He was our self-appointed leader. He was always doing dumb-ass stunts, and they usually involved near-death encounters.

One summer evening a bunch of us kids were sitting around on the Bouchards' lawn. We were hanging out, killing time until it was dark enough to play hide-and-seek. Lute got up and went inside. He reappeared armed with a bow and arrow. My older sister asked him, "What are you going to do with that? Play Robin Hood?"

"No," he replied, "I thought I'd do this." And with those words, he put an arrow on the string, pulled the bow to full draw, pointed it straight up into the darkening sky, and let that arrow fly.

This got the undivided attention of us gawking bystanders. We homed in on the Bouchards' open garage door about fifty feet away like a flock of pigeons. But not Lute. He stood there laughing, watching us go. The arrow came down with a whistling thud, quivering in the ground a dozen feet away from him. He walked over and yanked it out, grinning like an idiot. We all came out of the garage, and my sister lit into him.

"What are you trying to do, kill somebody? You big dumb weenie!"

"If I'm a big dumb weenie, then you guys are all Ta-Ta Weenies!" Lute replied.

"Ta-Ta Weenies?" my sister asked.

"Yeah," Lute replied, "As in Ta! Ta! You weenies!" And he launched the arrow again, straight up into the night sky to an instant replay of kids screaming and running for cover like their hair was on fire. But once again, not Lute. He stood there laughing like the moron we all knew he was. It missed him again by a margin of a dozen or so feet.

Over the course of the next few days, the term "Ta-Ta Weenie" came into vogue. It took on a life of its own. In extreme cases words such as brainless or dumb-ass preceded it. Soon it even replaced chowderhead as our favorite derogatory expression.

It spread through the neighborhood like wildfire. From early morning swimming lessons to evening Little League, kids were calling each other Ta-Ta Weenies at the drop of a hat. Mostly because it was just so much dang fun to say. Go ahead. Try it. I know you're going to.

And it had nice variations. It could be shortened up in a pinch. We could just call somebody a Ta-Ta—it would make them feel like they didn't deserve the full Weenie. And we could speed it up and give it kind of evil accent.

"You Tata Weeeenie!" It was very versatile.

It was during this fever pitch of popularity that the Ta-Ta Weenie Club was born. Lute appointed himself the Grand High Ta-Ta, and he held the number one position for the life of the club. Mercifully, that life was short.

The rules to join the Ta-Tas were simple. All you had to do was perform a feat of stupidity that proved you worthy of being called a Ta-Ta Weenie. The only drawback was what that feat would be. Because the Grand High Ta-Ta, along with other Ta-Tas, also known as survivors, decided that. At least two bona fide Ta-Tas in good standing had to witness you performing the qualifying feat.

The ceremonial Ta-Ta Weenie hat proclaimed that one of us had made it into the elite. It consisted of a triangle-shaped head covering made from newspaper. The hat had the recipient's officially assigned Ta-Ta Weenie Number scrawled on the side in red magic marker. It was a trendsetter. Lute scotch-taped a big black crow feather to his chapeau, then refused to let anyone else do likewise. He also made a strict rule that we had to wear our hats to the club meetings that were held in the haymow of our barn. Lute was quite the dictator; he ruled with an iron fist.

We built rooms randomly throughout the haymow, connected by the warren of tunnels we had constructed among the bales of hay. My father referred to them as Burmese tiger pits.

Slowly dismantling our rooms and tunnels each winter as he fed out the hay was a challenging prospect. It was like playing a lifesize game of Jenga with hay bales piled twenty feet high. He never knew which bale would be the kingpin and might bring the whole shooting match down on top of him.

We named each of our rooms. We even had the Ta-Ta Weenie Post Office for decoding and sending secret messages via the Ta-Ta Telephone, built with standard issue soup cans and lengths of string. We had the Ta-Ta Weenie Jail for insubordinate club members. And there was one we called the Fart Room. Personally, I would've much rather done hard time in jail then spend any time in the Fart Room, for obvious reasons. Lute could part your hair from across the room.

The Ta-Ta Weenie Club's membership expanded very quickly. It seemed the chance to serve such a worthy cause as the Ta-Ta Weenie's was just too good to pass up. We didn't care how embarrassing or dangerous the exploit might be, as long as it would let us join the ranks.

Sometimes we had to draw straws or do "potato man" to see who would have the honor of the selected challenge. Potato man being the agricultural version of eenie-meanie-minie-moe. The competition was that fierce. Buzzy Becktell was awarded the privilege of streaking the neighborhood Fourth of July Barbecue.

Streaking was a popular term for bare-ass running at public events. Buzzy, true to his name, buzzed through wearing only his PF Flyers and a Porky the Pig Halloween mask.

Unfortunately, his parents were at the barbecue, too, and his mother recognized his freckled ass when he leaped over the bonfire. A daring feat that Buzzy ad-libbed on the fly, and thus earned himself Ta-Ta Bonus points that shot his Ta-Ta Weenie number up three grades.

Buzzy's promotion did come with a price. His dad got hold of him and made quite an impression on Buzzy that he was not to do anything of that nature ever again. The impressions, of course, being on his freckled ass.

My assigned feat of stupidity to join the renowned Ta-Ta Weenies was one I suggested at the club board meeting one afternoon while inhaling as little as possible in the Fart Room.

We had a hay bale archery target set up on the edge of the field between the Bouchards and our other neighbors, the Yandows. Mrs. Yandow was one of the worst worrywarts in the county. She constantly complained about the archery target being nothing but an accident waiting to happen. We decided to end her waiting.

Our crack team of Ta-Ta Weenie Engineers designed a leather belt through which they twisted a little screw. Then they threaded the screw into the cut-off end of half an arrow. They strapped this apparatus to my bare chest. Over it I put my shirt. This feathered half of the arrow stuck through a hole in my shirt, which they'd doctored up with ketchup.

On the selected day, I staggered into Mrs. Yandow's kitchen, gasping like a guppy, and flopped onto the floor. I was really selling it. After all, the pride of the Ta-Ta Weenies was on the line, as well as my membership in the group.

Mrs. Yandow sat relaxing at her kitchen table, drinking coffee and reading the newspaper. We got the desired response. But our plan lacked an escape route. This shortfall resulted in my being dragged by my ear across the road to my house, with the arrow still sticking out of me. There, Mrs. Yandow made me explain to my parents what I had done.

They confiscated my bow and arrow for two weeks. Down but not out, during this period I learned how to make and throw a spear properly. Proving the old adage that every cloud does indeed have a silver lining.

My stellar performance qualified me for acceptance into the Ta-Ta Weenie Club. I was assigned the lucky Ta-Ta Weenie Number Thirteen. I can still see that number being written on my hat during the swearing-in ceremony. We all even teared up a bit. We held my ceremony in the Fart Room, as it was right after frank-and-bean night.

The last assignment carried out by two new recruits was one that sounded easy, but wrote the final chapter for the Ta-Ta Weenies. Skizzy Mayo and Meatball Brown were the next two vying for entry into our ranks. They were top candidates. Skizzy was the only person I ever knew who could drive a car to school while attending eighth grade. As for Meatball, well, I think his name says it all. He was shaped like one. He was what we called a light eater. If it was light, he was eating.

On a moonlit summer night Skizzy and Meatball, along with the Weenies that weren't under curfew, met at a cow pasture just a wagon race or so down the road from our house.

Skizzy and Meatball were each armed with a can of bright blue spray paint.

It was 1968, and Vermont was in the mist of debate about banning the use of billboards in our bucolic state. Being the civic-minded club we were, we decided to add our two cents worth to the argument.

It was Lute, our fearless leader, who'd come up with the idea of painting our club's name on the sides of cows. He was a prodigy. We'd agreed that the two recruits would put the letters "TA" on two cows and "WEENIE" on a third.

Lute gave them instructions before they climbed into the pasture. "You want to look for a good long, lanky one for the 'WEENIE' so you can be sure to get it all on her."

"How are we going to get them to line up in the right order?" Meatball asked.

"Try and pick out three that can read," our Grand High Ta-Ta replied.

Things actually went quite well at first. They got "TA" on both sides of two cows. However, unknown to us, the farmer had just recently put a bull in with his herd. And he was the big, long, lanky one the boys selected to display "WEENIE" on.

The bull wasn't too keen on the idea. He head-tossed Skizzy about twenty feet. This was beneficial for Meatball, because while the bull was punting Skizzy around the pasture, Meatball had time to roll out of the field under his own power.

While he was chasing Skizzy, fate stepped in. The bull inadvertently tromped down on a dropped paint can and broke the nozzle off. It sprayed bright blue paint all over his ball sack. He sported the worse known case of blue balls ever witnessed in the bovine world.

The next day, Lute called a club conference. We all met out by the pasture that afternoon. Lute said, "The first coat of paint on that bull's ball sack must be dry by now. I think we should select somebody to go in there and give it a second coat."

We looked at him like he was nuttier than a squirrel turd. It was at this point that Skizzy made a motion to disband the club. Meatball seconded it. We voted by raising our hands. As I stood by the fence with my hand raised and watched, the two cows we'd painted lined up perfectly to read "TA! TA!"

The motion carried. We all turned and fanned out for home.

~

THE IRON HORSE

In the winter of '67 we were the first family on our road to
buy a snowmobile. It was a 1966 Ski-Doo Olympic with a
fourteen-horsepower motor. On good flat ground with a stiff
tail wind, it could go almost thirty-five miles per hour. An
unheard-of speed on snow at the time. The next year, Dad
bought a brand new ten-horsepower model that could almost
hit thirty.

During the winter those machines made us more popular than a punch bowl at a barn dance. I think half the reason
Dad bought the second one was to free up the first one so that
he might actually get a chance to drive it. Because he loved to
drive things.

The Old Man, being a first-rate mechanic, had an obses-
sion for putting motors, wheels, even skis on just about anything. He figured if something was good standing still, it would
always be even better if you made it go.

This philosophy produced the wood splitter we could drive from one pile of wood to the next. And he once turned a hand-crank corn sheller into a motorized tornado that shot corn out with the speed of a Gatling gun.

A few days after he brought the snowmobile home, there wasn't a patch of snow left within a half-mile radius of our house that hadn't been flattened by that Ski-Doo's track. It didn't matter to us that we were just going around in circles. We were going. This behavior led to the Old Man saying, quite loudly, as he was pouring the umpteenth gallon of gas into the machine, "You give kids something with a motor on it, and they'll go ape- shit."

I don't know how long it took mankind to figure out how to hitch a cart behind a horse. It took us kids about three days before we realized that we could tow things behind that snow-mobile. We began with a flying saucer on a good long rope. Then multiple saucers on good long ropes.

This turned into a motorized winter version of roller derby, a competition to see who could stay on their saucer the longest while being towed at breakneck speed around the neighbors' fields. We soon hitched toboggans and even skiers to the back of that snowmobile.

Hands down, the best thing we ever hitched up behind our snowmobile was a behemoth of a three-legged tricycle invented by the Old Man that we named the Iron Horse. He made it during the summer before our second season of snow-mobiling.

Dad took an old motor-scooter frame and removed the tires. On the rear he made an axle about five feet long on the ends of which he attached the upturned corner of bus bumpers as skis. They looked sort of like outriggers on a canoe or the dugouts you see those natives paddling like crazy on "Hawaii-Five-O." He put another one up front in the center, attached to the steering column.

The Iron Horse weighed about half a ton. To keep it as light as possible, the seat was a bare two-by-four about four feet long that the rider straddled.

This actually worked out okay. It made the rides short because your ass couldn't stand sitting on that unpadded board for more than five or ten minutes. This kept the time kids had to wait for a ride manageable. And three or four kids fit easily on that seat.

We attached this monstrosity to a thirty-foot rope that let us zig-zag along behind the snowmobile. If the snowmobile stopped too quickly, or if it was on a downhill run, the rope also allowed the Iron Horse riders to pass the snowmobile. Because there was no braking mechanism whatsoever on the thing. Dad was good at making things go; he was only fair at making things stop.

And you'd better have a white-knuckle grip onto something if we were riding on the Iron Horse and there was any slack in the rope. Usually a big jerk would suddenly take up the slack. Especially if a big jerk was driving the snowmobile.

The hours we spent riding on the Iron Horse piled up faster than the snow that year. Neighborhood kids would come bailing out of their houses like they were on fire when they heard the snowmobile start up.

There could easily be a dozen of us waiting for a turn. We even strapped the Old Man's six-cell flashlight to the handle-bars for night riding. That was my brother George's idea, and he took the heat for it when Dad went to use his beloved flashlight and the batteries were deader than a doornail.

One Saturday afternoon we were trying to catch some air with the beast by towing it full throttle over a snowdrift in the neighbor's field. This wasn't meeting our expectations because the weight of the Iron Horse made it plow right through the drift. The Old Man was watching us, and he came up with a solution to the problem. He liked to say that if you came up with enough ideas, sooner or later you were bound to get a good one. Unfortunately, this wasn't one of those times.

He went and got an old eight-foot sheet of plywood and leaned it onto a couple of 55-gallon drums. Next, he shoveled a bunch of snow onto it. Viola! We now had a doozy of a launching ramp. Sort of like the kind water skiers use.

We had to draw straws to see who would be the first test pilot. My brother George won. Or lost, depending how you look at it. Now, why any father would allow his twelve-year-old offspring to jump from a four-foot-high ramp on such a metal monstrosity as the Iron Horse is one hell of a good question. And that was the question the Old Man had to answer when my mother came home from shopping and saw what we were doing.

And, boy oh boy, she got even madder when she found out that the Old Man had been the second one to go over the jump once he saw that his son had survived. I never got a chance to jump it. Mom stopped the fun before I got my turn.

Thank God! Because I was scared to death to try it, but I sure didn't want to be called chicken. I was ten years old and really wanted to see what eleven was like. George got to jump it twice. His second run led us to almost changing its name from the Iron Horse to the Nutcracker due to his abrupt contact with the two-by- four when he landed that jump.

Late in the winter we had a good thaw and then a hard freeze. The snow developed a three-inch-thick crust, which allowed the snowmobile and the Iron Horse to stay on top of it. We could go just about anywhere. The Old Man decided this would be a good time to take George, our neighbor's kid, Craiger, and me for a ride on the hillside pasture across the road.

We were going up the hill just fine until we got to the edge of the woods and the Old Man turned and went sideways to the grade. As we were on a long rope, we did not go sideways to the grade. We swung downhill like a pendulum on top of that hard crust until we were even with the snowmobile but on a ninety degree angel to its course. Then the Iron Horse hogged into the crust and rolled a couple times.

I was the lucky one. I was on the downhill end of the horse and went off backwards. The most painful part was my face crashing through the crust of the snow. George and Craiger got banged up fairly well but were able to limp away from the crash.

The Iron Horse didn't get a scratch. The Old Man chewed out George, who was steering, for not following behind him properly. Apparently the Old Man thought the law of gravity would be suspended on his say-so.

It wasn't that long before we got tired of towing things behind the snowmobile. As we got older and into high school, we had more important things to do. We even got sick of going around in circles.

But as I look back, I realize that there are a lot of things in life that have us going around in circles. And sometimes those circles bring us back around to something good and wholesome.

A little while ago I was out in our barn with my four-year-old grandson. He pointed over in the corner and asked, "What's that, Grandpy?"

"That," I said, "is a 1972 Ski-Doo Olympic. It used to be my dad's. We haven't used it in years. It'll need a bit of fixing up before we could use it."

His eyes got wide as he asked, "Can we fix it up and use it Grandpy?"

I looked at the excitement in his face and the familiar lines of the old machine. I could almost hear the squeal of kids and the smell and sound of a two-cycle gas engine as it purrs along over the snow-covered fields.

"That's a peach of an idea," I smiled. "But if we get her going, we're going to need a flying saucer and a good long piece of rope."

BEARS AND PINK BLANKETS

We always had a camp. Not some cute little chalet nestled by a flowing mountain stream. No, sir. It was a cobbed-together hovel. The original version was an asphalt, shingle-sided shack with a fair amount of exposed tar paper. Maybe fourteen by twenty feet, it was mostly made from apple crates and pallet lumber and any other scrounged timber found at hand.

The camp squatted on a half acre of land that the Old Man bought as partners with my Uncle Deke back in the '50s for $25. It was located on a dead-end, dog path of a road. I guess it really wasn't a dead end if you had a four-wheel drive and very few brains. If you kept going past our camp, it did come out in the back of Pratt's cow pasture. That involved going alongside a string of beaver ponds that encroached on the road and then across a brook on an old rickety bridge that was shy most of the planking.

The camp had a lean-to shed on the side that served as a catchall for things that we had given up on at home. An old lawn mower that ran some of the time, if you didn't pull the starter cord out of it first. A cross-cut saw that was duller than hell with one handle missing. Old hibachis, and washbasins with holes in them. Things that weren't of much use but, by god, let's not throw them away. We can bring them up to camp.

That my dad was a child of the Great Depression was evident by the useless junk brought to camp, junk that he couldn't part with, selected from the scads of stuff squirreled away at home. And the nut didn't roll far from the tree.

When his father, my grandpa, was moved to the nursing home, he had six pairs of new bib coveralls in his bureau drawer. The pair he was wearing was covered with so many different colored patches, it was hard to tell what the original color was. When asked why he didn't wear a new pair, he said he was saving them for later. He was eighty-six.

That first old camp was a special place for us kids. One of the neat things about it was that it had cardboard for the ceiling. Not Sheetrock. Sheetrock costs money. Cardboard can be had for free. It was the best feature of the camp for us kids, because it made for great entertainment. It allowed us to shoot through it with our BB guns at the mice scurrying over our heads at night. This developed a skill that would come in handy as we got older. Shooting by sound, in the dark, at moving targets is a fair description of opening morning of deer season.

The camp was a place that offered a different ambiance from our home. Hoards of black flies through June. Clouds of mosquitoes and no-seeums in July and August. And let's not forget the deer flies the size of pelicans. They would arrive in such numbers when we pulled into camp that we were afraid to get out of the vehicle. That is, if we were lucky enough to be inside a vehicle. Most times we would take Dad's pickup truck.

As we were getting ready to go, we would fight to see who would get to ride in the back. Days before a scheduled trip, we'd have called dibs for seats. Dad had strapped some old bus seats in the back bed of the truck. This was the woodchuck version of a child safety seat and the closest thing to an air-conditioned ride we would ever get.

Being the youngest, I would usually lose out and have to ride up front. I would feel better about it as we arrived at camp. I would watch in amusement as the clouds of deer flies descended onto my siblings as we pulled up. In front, we would have the windows rolled up and the doors locked. The Old Man would sit in the truck for a few minutes before he would get out and unlock the camp. By then, most of the deer flies would be off circling and biting the kids running and screaming alongside the camp.

"Nothing better than having some deerfly decoys to take the heat off," he would say.

He firmly believed that deer flies prefer the meat of sweaty, greasy kids. And any deer fly biting a kid was one that wasn't biting him. If my mom was along, he wouldn't be able to torture us too long. She'd roll her eyes and sit there for a bit and then declare that he'd abused the kids enough and to get out of the truck.

Food always tasted better at camp. Even a burnt hot dog had more flavor than at home. So did peanut butter sandwiches and Cheesies that left our fingers orange. Cherry Kool-Aid or root beer to wash it all down. My mom would make a large batch of root beer every spring. She would lay the bottles on their sides under my bed to age. Once, for a bit too long. In the middle of the night a couple of bottles exploded with a bang that woke the whole family up. I was gun-shy for a week.

At camp we took full advantage of the natural larder that was free for the taking. Fat native brook trout swam in the beaver ponds and alder-covered brooks that fed those ponds. There were service berries in June. Raspberries in July. Blueberries and blackberries in August.

Chokecherries and wild apples in September. Hazelnuts and butternuts that we took home and dried for later. By the end of the summer, I would be crapping like a bear.

And bears there were. Some of the local folks occasionally used an old dump in a ravine next to the road a few hundred yards from camp. One late summer day my friend Kirk Perkins, my dog Smokey, and I were walking by it and heard something grubbing around down at the bottom. Kirk picked up a rock and chucked it down the ravine at the noise. We'd figured it was a porcupine. The biggest bear I'd ever imagined in all the bear-filled stories told at camp stood up and gave us a real mean look.

We stood there gawking for about as much time as it takes for a fart to fade in a high wind. Then we both lit out for camp like somebody'd shot a starter's pistol. There was a good downhill grade for the last seventy-five yards to the camp, and I swear my heels were coming up by my ears when we heard heavy panting and a galloping pounding behind us. Old Smoke came blasting right up between us. If it was possible for twelve-year-old kids to have a heart attack, consider it done.

Of course, nobody would believe that we saw a bear. The next weekend, when bear season started, Windy Mallard's bear dogs took a bear track from the dump. They chased that bear through Snipe Ireland Swamp and fought it to a standstill on the backside ledges. Only the big ones will stand and fight, and Windy barely got there in time to save his dogs. The bear fought his way free before Windy could get a clear shot into him and got away. He said it was a monster- sized bruin.

Fall and hunting seasons always arrived together. Hunting started with bears and squirrels on the first of September, then partridge and rabbit season on the last Saturday of the month. The high point of the fall would be the deer rifle season. Starting a couple Saturdays before Thanksgiving, it was supposedly the reason that the camp was built. But I know of only one legal deer ever shot there.

There were others that weren't reported. Like the time when Mutt Summers was driving back to camp from a beer run and saw a doe caught in a barbed-wire fence. The poor thing was blind. Some fool had shot her in the face with a load of birdshot. All Mutt had in the truck to dispatch her was a ball-peen hammer. It wasn't a pleasant job, but one that had to be done. My dad and his buddies at camp teased Mutt for breaking the law: Everybody knows that ball-peen hammer season doesn't start till after rifle season.

My Old Man and his buddies didn't push the woods too hard. Visiting friends' camps or having friends stop by theirs was all they were really hunting for. Playing some card games and drinking some beer. Smoking rank- smelling cigars they weren't allowed to smoke at home. Getting up early and staggering out into the dark, cold woods wasn't something they were aching to do. But on opening day it was camp tradition to be out there before dawn.

As a rule, they didn't allow kids on opening weekend. Kids would go up on the second weekend. On one particular Friday night before opening day, my Old Man and three of his friends were at camp and having a festive time. They realized as they went to bed that nobody had brought an alarm clock.

"Don't worry," Mutt said. "I'm part Indian. I'll set my internal hunting alarm for four o'clock sharp." And they all collapsed into their bunks.

When Mutt woke up later to take a leak, he dug out his watch. Through eyes fogged from Schlitz, he checked the time.

"Holy Moly!" he shouted, "Time to get up! It's five after four! Everybody up!"

They all moaned and groaned and farted their way out of their bunks. Mutt started coffee and got to work on breakfast. It was camp tradition to have a good hearty breakfast before they soldiered out to try to slay a buck.

Mutt was the cook at camp. He never strayed too far out in the woods. His sense of direction was terrible, despite his claim of Indian lineage. In truth, he'd get lost trying to find a church steeple in a cornfield.

This morning Mutt tore into making breakfast at a fevered frenzy. He stuffed all his hunting buddies with eggs and bacon and sausage, with home fries and toast and scalding-hot coffee that could float a half-inch nut.

Everybody got all decked out in their hunting duds. Mutt stopped to put his watch on and checked the time again. It was then he noticed it said 2:15. What he'd thought was 4:05 was actually 1:20. It was the classic case of being all dressed up and nowhere to go.

During the discussion while they waited for legal shooting light they made a momentous decision. One that would ease the burden and fuss on opening day forever. They came up with numerous reasons for the new rule. What if they went visiting and some thief came and stole their cherished weapons? And if by some miracle one of them actually shot a deer, then what? They would have to gut it out, drag it to camp. Skin it and cut it up and package it. It was way too much hassle. When they took the vote, it passed unanimously: No more guns at camp. The deer never even noticed.

For us kids, going to camp in the summer was fun. Going to camp in the winter was an adventure. On one winter weekend, just Mom, Dad, and I were going up to camp for some snowmobiling. We had our two snowmobiles in the truck that we'd loaded the night before. The morning broke colder than a polar bear's toenails, well below zero.

"Better keep the brass monkeys in this morning," the Old Man said with deep satisfaction as he fired up the old GMC pickup. We had gone about five or six miles down the road when my mother said, "I smell something."

"Oh, you're always smelling something, Woman," the Old Man replied.

"No, I smell something burning!" she insisted.

As I was sitting in the middle, between them, I had a good view of the expression of realization that appeared on my Old Man's face as he slammed on the binders and bailed out of the truck. His eyeballs sort of stretched wide, and his eyebrows shot up.

Once we'd come to a screeching halt, we saw the whopping stream of black smoke coming from under the hood. The Old Man jumped out and popped the latch and raised the hood, and a huge mushroom cloud of smoke billowed out.

He reached in and grabbed the two corners of an old pink blanket he'd put over the engine the night before to keep it warm. Unfortunately though, it was caught on something. So rather than pull it out, what he did was fan it up and down, releasing big black clouds of smoke at each tug. It looked like he was trying to send smoke signals to a neighboring tribe.

He finally got that blanket loose, threw it onto the snowbank, and did a little war dance on it to snuff the flames out. He jumped back into the truck and we tore off like a big ass bird and neither my mother nor I said a word. We drove on in silence. Well, I started to say something, but my mother elbowed me in the ribs.

We had a peach of a day snowmobiling. And when we drove home past the scene of the crime, the charred remains of the blanket were still smoking! My mother and I both looked at each other and just lost it.

When we caught our breath, I said, "I thought there would be some Indians around it waiting for a pow wow." And we went off on another laughing jag. Even the Old Man joined in.

That old pink blanket, like a lot of life's possessions, had a variety of uses. From keeping us warm and snug when it was nice and new, to making us smile and laugh when it was old and tattered and on fire.

I never had a disappointing trip to camp. The destination was known, but the journey was always a crap shoot. Like cranking along on a jack-in-the-box, lulled by the tune until something pops out to surprise you. Quite similar to the life I've led. With the music forever changing cadence with the unexpected encounters along the way.

THE SWINGING TREE

In my youth, summer didn't last as long as it does now. Summer's sweet days seemed to tumble by as quickly as a row of dominoes falling, until the last leaned up against the ominous schoolhouse door.

In early June when I hightailed it down the doorsteps of the school, it felt like eternity stretched in front of me before I'd have to slink back to social studies and vocabulary classes, math problems and P.E. I always thought Physical Education was uncalled for anyway. I needed more exercise like Custer needed more Indians.

At home I had to do chores to earn my keep. They changed throughout the seasons. During the summer, I could count on mowing the lawn and weeding the garden. Doing those chores earned me bonus money on top of my regular fifty cents a week allowance.

Lawn mowing was especially lucrative, depending on which lawn I mowed. Our front lawn was rather small. One of our side lawns had a ditch along it that was a pain in the ass to mow. The lawn on the other side was huge. And then there was the back lawn that ran down to and around the barn and tool shed.

My dad didn't believe in riding lawnmowers. Nearly everything else on the farm was motorized and drivable. But he figured as long as he had a Lawn Boy push mower and two sons with working legs, a riding mower wasn't needed. When we asked why we couldn't get one, his reply was, "It's the best way to teach you boys that life ain't all romance."

We got our workouts in lots of other ways, too. Weeding rows of sweet corn was piecemeal work. Ten cents a row, and no hoeing allowed. We had to pull the weeds up by the roots, and Dad wanted to see them, roots and all, in the middle of the row, before he would dole out your dime. This meant hands-and-knees weeding.

Luckily, we didn't have to do this work all day long, which left enough time for more important endeavors. There was a flock of anywhere from four to ten neighborhood kids who hung out together fairly consistently throughout the summer. More could be drummed up if needed, say for a baseball game. We'd play games that sometimes went on for days. Nine innings? Ha! That game is for wusses. In our neighborhood, first team to score one hundred runs got the bragging rights.

We set up a ball diamond on our big side lawn. My dad even made us a backstop to keep us out of his garden. Balls that cleared Route 117 on the fly were a home run. One bounce in the road was a triple; rolled across, a double. We hit an occasional car.

Hitting a car was an out. As in get the hell out of there as quick as possible.

When we weren't playing baseball, we found plenty of other things to keep us busy. Building tree forts went in and out of fashion. If one group of kids started building one, then another group would have to cobble one together, too. We hoarded and fought over scraps of lumber like dogs over a bone.

Good, straight nails were few and hard to come by. My dad had old coffee cans full of different-sized nails, all bent and rusty from one thing or another that he'd dismantled. He'd let us have them on shares. If we straightened them out, we could keep half. Our fingers would take a pounding, and we finally realized we were actually trading fingernails for tree-fort nails.

In summer, our time was our own, and we made the most of it. Even when we were resting between exploits, our minds were working on what we were going to play next. And that's what this was. Play.

When spent old geezers admonish today's young folk about being glued to their electronic devices and not going out to play, this is what they're talking about: doing the things that kids do when they're left to use their own wits and imagination. It's a crying shame to see kids today mesmerized by some electronic device, staring at a dinky little screen and twitching their fingers and thumbs.

Lute Bouchard mesmerized us. Lute was the guy who made a massive slingshot out of an old tire inner tube for flinging tomatoes. He taught us how to chuck spears through the open doors of boxcars on passing freight trains. And it was Lute who showed us how to light farts with a match without burning our asses. He was our go-to guy.

Damn near a prodigy.

So it was on a fateful day during the summer of 1966, one hot, glorious summer afternoon, that Lute; his younger brother Twitch; my brother, George; Ricky Hawley; and I were out playing.

We somehow ended up down by a big oak tree, about two hundred yards from our house in Hawley's horse pasture. The tree was a huge. It was about five feet in diameter. It was the largest white oak tree that I would ever see in my life. It went up for about ten feet and then branched out in massive limbs and an immense crown that seemed to take up about half an acre. It sat about three quarters of the way down a steep hill-side with a small brook at the bottom. The other side of the brook bank rose up a few feet and then flattened out for a bit before the railroad fence and the train tracks.

Where it was and it's unique shape made it the special place that it came to be. It was tucked out of site and hearing from adults. A place for kids. And it's position on the hill-side turned out to be the key to us having the swingingest of all swings. The first time on it took your breath away. It took courage. It was like going off the high dive at the swimming pool.

One of the oak's big long limbs grew out towards the side of the hill and came down to within a few feet of it before it curved upward. It resembled a bent index finger beckoning all kids to climb it. We were powerless to resist. We all shinnied up that low branch and perched like jaybirds in its big branches. It was Ricky who first suggested a swing.

"Hey, Lute," Ricky said as he leaned back against one of the oak's enormous branches. "Wouldn't it be neat if you could get a rope over that big limb right there and swing out over the brook?"

"You'd need one hell of a long piece of rope to reach the ground," Lute replied, "but I guess you'd swing like a hairy ape if you could get one and tie it up there."

Lute was as close to a hairy ape as we had; we figured he should know. At fourteen, he could have grown sideburns and a mustache if his mom had let him. But his mother was a devout Catholic, and she said she wasn't spending good money to send Lute to a Catholic school so he could look like "a hairy heathen."

"It's a mathematical fact that the length of the rope will tell you the distance of your swing," Twitch chimed in. "All we have to do is measure the distance from—"

"Will you shut the hell up with your goddamned mathematical calibrations so I can think!" Lute interrupted. "You know how numbers make my head hurt."

Lute was quite proficient with his cussing when out of earshot of an adult. At home he'd have his tongue scrubbed with a bar of Lava soap if he even rhymed something with a swear word. He could go from longshoreman to altar boy in the same breath if an adult, or a squealer, approached.

A squealer was a kid who hadn't yet realized that lying to your parents was permissible and sometimes demanded. Usually a young kid or a girl. And we never knew who would be a squealer until we got into deep trouble. Kee-Kee Fezzel, a neighborhood kid, was one we had to be careful around. He was only five or six and damn near invisible. He would willingly give up any information under the slightest cross-examination.

"I know where we can get a rope. A long freaking rope about an inch thick," said Ricky. "My dad has one hanging up in the rafters in the garage."

"Think he'd miss it if it suddenly disappeared?" Lute wondered. "I could just ask him if we could borrow it for a while," Ricky said. "Really? Are you shitting me?" Luke had other plans. "I say just 'borrow it' permanent-like."

"Heck," Ricky said, "It's been there as long as I can remember. I bet he'd let us use it. I'll go ask him."

"Go ahead, dumbass," Lute scoffed. "I'm a bit disappointed in you to see this honest streak coming out."

Ricky came back about twenty minutes later with a huge rope draped over his head and shoulders. He slid down the hill and stopped at the trunk of the tree, then heaved the rope off over his head and flopped to the ground, panting like a dog. That rope probably weighed more than he did.

"You got it!" Lute said. "So, your old man agreed?"
"I never asked him." Ricky was still gasping for breath. "He was on his back, pounding on something under the kitchen sink, and I didn't want to bother him right then. I figured he wouldn't mind, after all."

"Good thinking," said Lute. "It's just what I would've done. Now shinny your ass up there and tie it to that limb."

"Are you nuts?" Ricky had had enough. "I got the rope for us. Somebody else can shinny their ass up there."

We all decided that it would only be fair if we randomly picked a volunteer. Some thought we should do Potato Man. Others thought eenie-meanie-minie- moe. George liked his chances drawing straws. The debate raged on.

"Oh, great jumping Geronimo!" shouted Lute. "I'll climb

up there my own self, just so I don't have to listen to any more of your bitching and whining!"

Our stalling had worked. Lute swung the coil of rope over his head and shoulder, then grappled up that limb and out onto the huge branch like Cheetah the Chimp on that Tarzan show.

Once he got it tied to the limb, we made a loop in the end of it about a foot off the ground to stick a foot in. We kept backing up the hill as far as we could so we could swing farther. Once again, it was Lute, our fearless leader, who, with no discussion at all, came up with a scary, wonderful idea. He climbed up that limb that came down near the ground, turned and sat facing the swing, and said, "Toss me the rope."

We thought he was kidding. George tossed him the rope. As Lute slid his foot into the loop, Ricky started, "You ain't really going to go from—"

With a blood-curdling "Yeehaw!" suddenly Lute swung out like a freaking wild man. We all scrambled to be the one who would get up the limb next.

It was like a ride at the fair, but it didn't cost a dime. We would sail out over the brook so far we could almost high-five the engineer on a passing train. When we went over the brook we were about eight feet above it, and about twenty feet in the air at the end of the pendulum.

It wasn't long before we were trying stupid shit on that swing. If you knew how to pump the swing, you could reach back with one hand and whack the limb you swung off of. Or go from a standing position on a twelve-inch-diameter limb about eight feet off the ground on a steep hillside. This meant having to forgo the foot loop and just hang on for dear life.

The Swinging Tree became our hangout. It wasn't uncommon to have eight or ten kids down at the Swinging Tree. Sometimes more. All different ages, too. From six to sixteen, boys and girls. I recall seeing first kisses and fistfights. Sometimes between the same two people. Sips of a piss-warm beer and the smell of cigarette smoke. And learning new words that I had only a vague idea of what they meant. I did know enough not to repeat them at home.

But Kee-Kee Fezzel didn't. One Sunday night at the end of summer when his mother told him to get ready for his weekly bath, he looked her in the eye and said, "Go suck a wet one, Ma."

Once she'd grilled it out of the little rat-bastard as to where he learned such language, she got on the horn with the other parents in the neighborhood. And so Mr. Hawley made his oldest boy, Buddy, climb up the tree and cut the rope down.

But I still can close my eyes and be on that swing. Still feel the slight gasp of my breath as I slid off the limb and dropped down over the brook. I can recall that light-as-air feeling in the pit of my stomach as I flew into the bright-blue summer sky. Then, at the end of my arc, for that brief second as I hung in mid-air, time stood still. Life's ups-and-downs sure were a lot simpler when I was a kid.

~

Hold On to Something

My dad worked as a bus mechanic for forty-three years. But his mechanical abilities didn't stop at buses. He referred to himself as being "mechanically inclined." I took it to mean that he could fix or build anything he had a mind to.

The list of equipment he had at varying times covered a broad range of uses. At the top of his list was his 8N Ford tractor. He believed a farm couldn't and shouldn't be run without one. He even made a tractor from scratch by using a Jeep rear end and a Wisconsin motor.

We had an old Chevy C-60 dump truck and a Drott excavator when he was in his pond building phase. We ended up keeping them forever just because they turned out to be so darn handy to have around.

Hydraulic woodsplitters were a piece of cake for him to build. He even made a few for friends. And what's a woodsplitter if there isn't a conveyor to take the wood away or move it into a shed or basement.

Then there was haying equipment. The first baler he got was a monster of an International Harvester that spit a bale out about six foot long and weighed a ton. It took two men and a boy to lift them.

We kids loved the old baler because it was so huge it even had a four-foot-long seat on the side for passengers. It was the noisiest, dustiest, hottest place you could imagine on a hot, humid summer day, which most days haying were. The little 8N Ford tractor could only tow the behemoth of a baler at a snail's pace. But all we cared about was that we were riding on something. We'd fight for a spot on the seat.

There was a sickle bar hay mower for the 8N Ford. A side delivery rake for putting hay into windrows for baling. Also, an antique hay tedder that was made for horses. It was ground driven by the wheels turning. If it was pulled any faster than a horse would walk, it'd shoot the hay into the next field. Conveyors weren't only for wood. We had one for hay bales, too, to take them up into the barn.

There were disc harrows and plows and walk-behind gasoline rototillers for the garden. We had a couple of manure spreaders. The first one he got was a chain flail type that threw the manure out the side of it. When he finished spreading a load with it, he remarked how the manufacturer would always stand behind it.

We had a place down over a bank in the back of a pasture where worn-out equipment would go to retire. My dad called it his outside tool shed. It couldn't be seen from the road or house. But usually we had enough stuff kicking around the yards and barn that it looked like we tried to have an auction and nobody showed up.

So I wasn't lacking at all for motorized entertainment when I was a kid. We most always had something to ride with a motor on it. I'm grateful that my dad taught me to drive things, starting when I was quite young. His philosophy was that if your arms and legs were long enough to reach the control levers and pedals, you were old enough to drive it.

By far and away, one of the best contraptions that the Old Man ever came up with was the Bush Buggy. It came a few years after the doodle bug wore out. I was so young, I can barely remember the doodle bug. But I'll never forget the Bush Buggy.

We had recently purchased an adjoining twenty-two acres of land at our deer camp in West Bolton. He wanted something at camp to ride around on. Heaven forbid he might have to walk. The dune buggy fad was just heating up; people near beaches and sand dunes and out in western states were taking Volkswagen Beetles and retrofitting a fiberglass open-top body onto them.

Well, we didn't have any sand dunes to speak of. And Dad didn't want, nor could afford, a fiberglass body. He had his own idea on how to build it. After stripping the VW down to the frame, he took his trusty Saws-All and cut twenty-eight inches out of the middle of the car and welded it back together. This shortened the wheel base and allowed her to go over rough ground without getting hung up. It also shortened the turning radius. She could turn on a dime and give you nine cents change.

Just to be clear, Dad always referred to his vehicles in the female gender. He was not being a male chauvinist. It was a sign of affection and respect. Such as for your mother, wife, family, flag, apple pie, and the loyalty of a fine dog. It's a habit that I picked up too and still enjoy.

When he shortened the wheel base, he had to do away with the back seat area. But he didn't get rid of the long rear-bench seat. He removed the two front bucket seats and put the bench seat in where the front ones were. Now he could fit three people in the front.

There was still room for a cargo box just behind the front seat and it was about three feet wide by four feet long by two feet deep. You could also carry a couple more kids in that. Maybe three if they was fun sized. Kids could also stand in the box and hold onto the roll bar that he placed right behind the front seat.

It had bus bumper fenders that were on top of the tires and turned downward so the curve near the end of the bumper was following the roundness of the tire. He put these over both front and back wheels. He added headlights, and one loud freaking horn.

The Old Man had somehow got hold of a set of horns from the Ethan Allen Firing Range. They were used to warn of impending Gatling gun fire. They had the gun beat by a wide margin.

He taught a lot of us kids to drive a standard shift with the Bush Buggy. Some successfully. I have one sister that still can't drive a hen off a nest. I recall the time Dad was teaching her the difference between the clutch, brake, and gas pedals.

They went tearing through the squash patch, knocked down the pasture fence, and almost pitched down into the gully as Dad was screaming, "Brake! Brake! Hit the BRAKES!"

He immediately took it back to the workshop and put an engine kill switch on the passenger side. He even put a label over it. In large lettering it read, "Panic Button." Named so because Dad said he'd never felt such panic in his life. And he'd been on four war patrols on a sub in the South Pacific during WWII.

He was some proud of his invention. A Volkswagen Beetle, unlike most cars, has the engine in the rear. This puts the weight from it directly over the rear drive wheels. He swore that it could go more places than a Jeep, and proved it.

The road past our camp eventually ran alongside a network of beaver ponds. One of which encroached quite heavily on the road for a hundred yards or better. It was a formidable obstacle for any rig to make it through.

The local natives tended to avoid it when they could, but this one time, Windy Mallard, who lived up on the corner of the road as it turned down to our camp, was back in there looking for his lost coon hound. He got his Jeep buried to the floor boards. He walked up and got his dad and his Jeep and a stout chain. They got that one stuck as well.

They walked down to Pratt's farm and roped Sonny Pratt into coming with his tractor. Sonny planted that tractor in line with the two trucks. So he went back to the farm and got the biggest tractor that he had and was able to yank all three of them out to dry ground.

It was at this point that the Old Man and I showed up on the Bush Buggy. We pulled up and said our howdy-doos and the guys told us what had happened. We were able to squeak by them on the road and the Old Man turned and looked at me and smiled and said, "Hold on to something."

He matted the gas pedal and hit second gear just as we flew into the mud hole. We roosted up a tail of mud behind us that would have done any now-a-days mud bogger proud. When we got to the other side he turned it around and we hammered it back through. The Old Man was prouder than a dog with two tails. You'd of thought he'd just beat the Kaiser single handed.

We pulled up to the local boys watching us and loading up chain and he shut her down. Windy says, "That's a going rig you got there. I never thought you'd make it through. I wouldn't have believed it if I didn't see it my own self."

"Well," the Old Man replied, "you just got to have a steady arm and don't let off the foot feed. The best thing for it is to give it to her, full bore. Keeps the carbon from building up, too."

When they had all packed up and left, the Old Man decided to take a little spin around in the old field near the back of the pond before we headed back to camp. And it was while tooling around that field as he basked in the glory of his unbeatable Bush Buggy that he dropped into an unseen beaver channel. We were stuck and stuck good.

You could see the beads of sweat forming on the Old Man's brow as he paced around the buried Bush Buggy. Every now and again his gaze would shift from the Bush Buggy to the field edges to see if we were still alone in our predicament. There had to be some way to get it unstuck before somebody came and saw his invincible Bush Buggy mired in a measly frog pond. And he knew who he would have to ask for help: the same crew that had just left.

Well, not if he could help it. He'd exhaust all his options first.

"You slide over and drive. I'll get my shoulder into it and see if I can get the ass end of her up out of there. When I say 'give it to her,' you give it to her full throttle."

"Are you sure?" I said, "I think you'd—"

He cut me off before I could finish. "You just do what I say, Boy, and let me do the thinking."

He got squatted down behind the back of her, braced his feet as best he could, being standing in about six inches of water and a foot or so of mud, and he screamed out, "GIVE IT TO HER!!"

I tromped down on that gas pedal like I was trying to push it through the floorboards. We didn't move for a second or two, then she began to creep forward a little as we started to get onto better footing. I kept her glued right to the floor and glance over my right shoulder and could see a roost of mud shooting from behind the Bush Buggy like a fire hose. On one side. Something was blocking it on the other.

A mud encrusted creature that was the same size and shape of my Old Man emerged from behind the Bush Buggy when I finally let off the gas and coasted to a stop on dry ground. He stood there glaring at me as I slid over to the passenger side. All you could see were the whites of his eyeballs and he smelled like a wallowing moose.

"You said 'GIVE IT TO HER!'" I pleaded in defense of what I was sure was going to be a full-size ass chewing as I slid over onto the passenger side. He squished into the seat beside me.

"I sure did, Son. And you did a right proper job of it. Let's get the hell out of here before somebody comes by."

He looked at me and I could see the white of a smile come over his face. We both started laughing so hard I think I had tears running down my leg.

The next weekend we put a set of mud flaps on the Bush Buggy. The Old Man said it was like shutting the barn door after the horse was gone.

Most all of my friends didn't learn to drive till they were fifteen and got their learner's permit. I learned to drive a stick when I was eleven. At about the same time, I learned my dad wasn't infallible. That he wasn't really the unquestionable man of steel we all think our fathers are when we're young and look up to them with awe and wonder. He had strengths and weaknesses like we all do. I also learned another valuable lesson that day. One that my dad often repeated. The most dangerous part of any vehicle is the nut holding the steering wheel.

~

PEGGING ROCKS

I was an irrepressible rock chucker in my youth.

"Quit throwing rocks!" my Old Man would yell. "Keep it up and sooner or later, you'll be sorry."

He thought chucking rocks was as dangerous as lobbing hand grenades. If I had a nickel for every time he told me to quit chucking rocks, I'd have more nickels than I could chuck a rock at.

I think most boys are rock chucking junkies. There seems to be a naturally occurring function in a boy's arm so that if there is a good sized chucking rock close to hand, that arm will pick it up and chuck it at something.

We even came up with a term for it. "Chucking" was good, but we felt we needed something different. It was Lute Bouchard who decided that we would start pegging rocks at things. And if the expression was good enough for Lute, it was good enough for the rest of us. Lute was our self-appointed leader when I was on parole for the summer from Hardstick Elementary. Lute was the type of kid that others would follow, if only because he was fun to watch.

A bunch of us guys were walking along the railroad tracks about a stone's throw above and parallel to the river one summer day.

"Bet you can't peg a rock all the way down there and hit the river," said Lute. We all stopped at the same time and stooped for rocks like hens scratching for a June bug. That was one good thing about walking on the tracks; there was always a good supply of pegging rocks.

We all started pegging rocks for the river and listening for the splash. Since Lute was the oldest, he could peg one out there a ways. The rest of us—his younger brother Twitch, Craiger Yandow, my older brother George, and me—could just break the shoreline. We had just delivered a good steady barrage when this yahoo in chest waders and swinging a fishing pole came boiling out of the alders and pucker brush edging the river down below us.

"Hey, you damn kids! Quit throwing rocks down here!" he screamed at us, shaking both his fist and his pole.

"Cripes mister, we didn't know you were down there! And we're not throwing rocks! We're pegging rocks!" screamed Lute in our defense.

It was decided not to argue semantics and we started hoofing it down the tracks. But the incident really didn't surprise us. Most kids knew that trouble was just a stone's throw away when rock pegging was involved. We accepted the possibility only because we couldn't curb the habit.

We used to spend a fair amount of time walking on the railroad tracks. We weren't forbidden to be on the tracks, but we were warned to be careful. There was a spring running out of a pipe along the side of the tracks, not far from the gate crossing to our pasture. We kept an old tin cup hanging from the pipe so we could get drinks. That cold water was always welcomed on a hot summer day.

The overflow from the spring turned the ditches on either side of the tracks into a four-foot-wide swale of cattails. They were full of frogs and polliwogs, salamanders and turtles that naturally drew curious kids.

A new friend, Chris Moylan from Pinewood Manor, which was the housing development down the road, came over to visit one day. We were on the tracks engrossed in frog catching when we spotted a monster of a frog that we hoped would be the new champ in the frog jumping contest that was coming up on the Fourth of July Barbecue. We were on a curve of the train tracks where the sight distance was only a hundred yards or so due to the high banks on either side of the tracks.

We both felt a slight shaking of the ground and looked up at the same time to see the afternoon freight train barreling around the bend at us at what must've been the speed of sound because we hadn't heard a thing. That soon changed as the engineer laid on the horn, which only served to root us in place like deer in the headlights for a couple more seconds.

When the spell finally broke, it felt like the train was right on top of us. There was only one way to go and that was to jump the water-filled cattail ditch. I just cleared it, but Chris slipped on his launching lunge and stretched out in the slime-filled water as the line of boxcars thundered past us.

"As long as you're in there," I said, "fish around and see if you can find that old granddaddy croaker."

Thirteen-year-old boys can have quite a vigorous vocabulary of cuss words, and Chris, having moved up here from Boston, was no exception. He even pulled out a couple that had me puzzling over their meaning and filing them away for future use.

We wouldn't get in trouble for walking on the railroad tracks, but I bet our parents didn't have a clue as to how much walking on them we actually did or they might have put more restrictions in place. However, when it came to the train trestle, it was a different matter. It was strictly forbidden.

The train trestle was a half mile east of our house. It crossed about one hundred feet above the Winooski River and was about two hundred yards long. It had two emergency side boxes positioned at intervals along it for fools caught out on it when a train came.

And fools weren't hard to find. Lute and Dicky Hawley once stayed out in one of the boxes on a dare when a train came. The wind from the train passing by blew the baseball cap clean off Dicky's head and down into the river.

Walking on the trestle meant having to step on the railroad ties with the air gap between. Revealed between the gaps was the river far below and it gave a sort of dizzying effect to a person. But the view from the trestle was spectacular as it gave a vista of the river valley all the way from the new Country Dollar Discount Market next to Pinewood Manor almost to the town of Richmond miles down the line. And it sure was fun to peg rocks off of.

Of course, my other buddies weren't forbidden to go on the trestle. Or at least they didn't admit to it. So my brother George and I would stand on the edge of the trestle while our friends enjoyed the rock pegging privilege that the trestle afforded the brave and foolish.

One day we couldn't take it anymore. It started with just going out a few feet. The next thing we knew, we were out in one of those emergency boxes with pockets full of rocks, pegging them into the river to beat three of a kind.

No train came. The sky didn't fall. But a black cloud of guilt hung over us as my brother and I walked across the pasture home.

When we went in for supper and sat down at the table, my Mom said to George and me, "So, what did you two do today?"

"Oh, not a whole lot. Just this and that, hung around with the guys," said George.

"You weren't out on that train trestle, were you?"

I tried to swallow a spoonful of mashed potato that seemed to turn to sand in my mouth. She had us. She knew she had us. We knew she knew she had us. But there is always hope. Maybe she was just guessing. Maybe her intel was shaky. Maybe we could still weasel our way out of this predicament. George didn't bat an eye.

"No," he replied with the straightest face I'd ever seen. George was about as sharp as a bag of wet leather, but when it came to lying, he had balls the size of the King of Bayown.

"Liar!" my mom practically shrieked in triumph. "I was shopping down at the Country Dollar and saw you two."

"Are you sure it was us? It's quite a distance from there to the trestle," said George as he dug the hole deeper.

"It was you!" she barked, "I could see that yellow and red hat of your brother's quite clearly!"

Rats! I loved that hat. It was the type that Gilligan wore on Gilligan's Island except it had big yellow daisies on a red background. I figured Gilligan had a better chance of getting off that island than we had of getting out of this mess.

Now my Old Man, the high judge and executioner, spoke up.

"You couple of good-for-nothings. Get out of my sight and go to your room. You're grounded for a week. And no allowance either! What in the hell was so important that you had to go out on that trestle?"

We both answered in unison. "We were pegging rocks."

It isn't everybody that can peg a rock adequately can also skip a stone decently. And vice versa. Now you take Twitch for instance, Lute's younger brother. The sidearm motion needed for stone skipping just came naturally to him. It was almost like a muscle spasm. He could skip a stone from here to Christmas if the water was flat. But he couldn't hit the broad side of a barn if he was inside it rock pegging. I was only fair at both. Thus do we learn to live with life's shortcomings.

Now, skipping stones isn't the same as pegging rocks. If you were on a shoreline, be it a lake, pond, or river, you could look for a good flat skipping stone whilst you were pegging rocks. Thereby killing two birds with one stone, metaphorically speaking. However, if you were actually pegging rocks at birds while looking for a good skipping stone, it might actually be possible to get the full use of the phrase.

Growing up, we had a duck pen along a little stream before it went under the train tracks. We had an old doghouse for shelter in it and we kept a pair of mallard ducks. One spring the hen had a clutch of eggs that hatched out to thirteen ducklings. The only way you could've made them cuter is if they were wearing hats.

When I went to feed them one afternoon, the pen was littered with rocks from the tracks and every single duckling was dead. I'd seen some kids walking the tracks earlier. I noticed they were pegging rocks. I guess the glass insulators on the telegraph poles along the tracks weren't sporting enough. Or maybe they didn't have or need a reason.

I suppose we do a lot of things in life like we peg rocks. Just peg something out there without thinking much about the consequences. Even stepping out into places where we know we shouldn't and keep on pegging them. I guess my dad had it pegged. Keep it up, and sooner or later, you'll be sorry.

~

Fairly Stupid

My parents always made sure that I had certain chores to do to earn my weekly allowance. I would argue with them concerning my rate of pay. Some of my friends got their allowance and didn't have to lift a finger. This cut no ice with my Old Man.

"So what you're saying is that we should pay you your allowance just for breathing and eating? I don't see how that makes any sense."

"But Dad, Chris Moylan gets twice the allowance I do, and he doesn't have to take out the trash or feed the dogs or hand-pump water for the cows." A weak argument, but it was all I had.

"If ifs and buts were candy and nuts, we'd all have a Merry Christmas around here all the time now, wouldn't we?" he'd reply.

Finances would always come to the forefront as the summer wore on and the climax event of the season drew closer: the Champlain Valley Exposition, otherwise known as The Fair. One last blast of summer before the shackles of school were fastened back on.

We'd hoard pennies. Fights over two-cent returnable bottles could erupt between neighborhood kids. I'd mow the lawn if the grass grew half an inch.

"You mowed the front lawn again? Who the heck told you to do that?" my Old Man asked as he stepped out of his truck when he got home from work. I was waiting so I could put the bite on him for my pay.

"Nobody told me to. I thought it was looking kind of shabby. You've always told me to take some initiative around here. You got my fifty cents? I weeded four rows of corn, too. That's another forty cents."

He fished out his wallet and handed me a dollar bill. "Where's my change?"

I was ready for him. I reached into my pocket and handed him a penny. "Where's the rest of it?" he asked.

"Ten percent gratuity," I replied. "I did a bang-up job, if I do say so myself."

"I'm sure coming out the small end of the horn on this deal!" he griped as he shook his head and walked to the door with his lunch bucket. "Fleeced of a dollar before I can get in the door."

Because the coming of The Fair signaled the end of summer, I always wanted it to go out with gusto. The amount of money I could gather together determined how many rides at the fair I could go on. Also how much fried dough, greasy sausage, French fries, onion rings, candy apples, cotton candy, and other nutritious cuisine I could scarf down. Whether I could keep it down depended on which rides I went on.

Going on Kids Day saved the price of admission, but the crowd was large then, and the lines at the rides long. The ideal method was to go twice. Double your pleasure, and double your fun.

Go on Kids Day if you were under twelve or looked it. Then sneak in on another day, saving the cost of admission and thereby stretching your meager funds even further for rides and vittles.

Sneaking in was always exciting. There were a couple ways to go about it. One was to hook up with an older kid who had a driver's license and pack a few of us into the trunk of the car.

There were usually parking attendants flagging drivers to the designated parking areas. These guys would nab you if they could. But many of them were old and out of shape and weren't getting paid enough to chase after sprinting kids. If we could make it to the crowded midway, we were home free.

The car trunks of my youth had to be opened with a key. The trick was to have the driver slyly open the trunk as the guys inside held it mostly shut. Once the legal occupants of the car had wandered off, the hope was to slide out of the trunk and meander over to the midway unnoticed. Then there was the jack-in-the-box routine that is self-explanatory and was always a hoot.

Another way was to find a hole in the fence or to climb over it. There was a long stretch of fence that ran through the woods behind the Summit Street School. The fair staff couldn't fix the holes fast enough to stem the tide. And tide it could be.

We would use the saturation method, getting half a dozen or so of us together and hitting them with a wave of fence-busting teenagers. They couldn't catch all of us, and it was every man for himself. So we didn't have to outrun the guard, just the slowest kid in the group. We'd set a rendezvous time and place to meet up inside the fair for the successful participants and any slow kids who got caught and had to pay to get in.

Until I was nine or so I wasn't old enough to go around the fair by myself. I went with my parents and an older sibling or two. My parents always volunteered to work in the PTA food concession stand at the bottom of the grandstand. They would send me off with my older siblings and make us promise to walk through all the livestock barns and craft exhibits before we went on any rides. To us it felt similar to dragging us to church every Sunday. We had to pay penance before we could have any pleasure.

From the time I was ten years old I was allowed to go around the midway without supervision as long as I was with other kids. Quite often, it was somebody a bit older like my brother George or my cousin Donny and Kirk Perkins. Our parents thought we would be safer and wouldn't get in trouble if we were in a group. Another theory shot to hell. They didn't realize that one-up-man-ship and dares got us into more trouble than we ever could've by ourselves.

The sights, sounds, and smells of the fair seemed to be magnified as the sun went down. Carnies barked at passersby to take a twenty-five-cent shot at winning a ten-cent prize. Lights and sirens went off when some rube actually won something at a booth. The beat of the latest rock-and-roll songs blasted from speakers around the midway. Colored lights flashing off and on everywhere illuminated it all. But The fair in those days wouldn't have been complete without the hoochie-coochie girlie shows.

When the girls came out in the evening and danced on the podiums in front of their tent, the crowd out front would block the midway to a standstill. I'd seen more cotton on the top of an aspirin bottle than in the outfits those girls were wearing.

One summer when I was fourteen, I was at the fair on a hot, humid night with Kirk Perkins and my cousin Donny. We were glued to the dancers out front like mold on cheese.

"They're going to twitch it! They're going to twatch it! You pay three bucks, and you can watch it!" the carnie up front shouted to the crowd of gawkers bunched around the girls.

"They're going to shake it loose like a bucket of juice on a coooold frosty morning!" he continued, as one of the strippers gave a pretty darn good rendition of a belly dancer's jiggle.

"That's gotta be jelly because jam don't shake like that!" he yelled to the crowd that was hooting and hollering catcalls and whistling. Those girls were showing more meat than a butcher's window.

Donny and I dared Kirk to try to get into one of the girlie shows. He had big bushy sideburns and was quite husky from working on the farm. He considered himself a snappy dresser, too, and was all decked out in his best fair duds. He wore a fancy southwestern-style light blue shirt with flowers embroidered around a horseshoe and had a big silver peace sign hanging from a chain around his neck. The first couple buttons on his shirt were open, and the peace medal rested in actual chest hair. Brown corduroy bell-bottom pants and Dunham shitkicker boots completed his ensemble. He looked like a cross between Roy Clark on Hee-Haw and Elvis Presley before he blimped up.

Kirk still needed some convincing to get in line for the show.

"You scared to go in?" said Donny. "Afraid of what you might see? They don't bite, ya know."

"What don't bite? Oh, I know that! But what if somebody sees me in there? I could get in trouble."

"Nobody's going to squeal on you. They'd have to admit that they were in there too," I said.

Kirk finally agreed to give it a try, but only if Donny and I each kicked in a dollar apiece towards his ticket. I thought it was a highway robbery, but I sure did want to know what was going on in that tent.

Kirk bummed a cigarette from a guy just before he got in line and lit it up. He had it hanging from his lips as he got to the ticket booth and handed his money to a guy inside who barely even looked up at him. Kirk gave us a stupid grin as he walked inside the tent like he was entering the gates of heaven.

"Well, suck ol' Rose! He made it!" Donny said. "Hell, I'm going to sneak around back and see if I can get a look inside of that tent. Come on," as we heard the hurdy-gurdy music start up inside.

"Not me," I said. "I'll wait for Kirk out here."

"You chicken?!"

"Yes. Yes, I am. You go right on ahead, you stupid bastard."

I'd gotten in so much trouble over the years because of Donny and his weasely ways that I was finally smartening up.

Donny eased off to the side of the crowd and slid around the backside of the tent, from which the hooting, whistling, and cheering were getting louder. About five minutes later, Donny came staggering back out from behind the tent. He was drenched in mud and water, and smelled pretty bad.

"What the hell happened to you?!" I said.

He didn't answer other than to say, "Let's get the hell out of here." We walked off around the corner and between a couple of game booths.

"So what happened?" I asked again.

"Well, I snuck up to the wall of the tent and got down on my hands and knees and pried the tent up enough so I could get my head under it. I was laying there trying to figure out what I was seeing—"

"What were you seeing?" I interrupted. This was important.

"Well, there were a few guys in the way, but I was getting glimpses of that red-headed dancer we saw out front."

"You mean the ugly one?" I said.

"You think she's ugly? Well, you ain't seen her stripped right down to her pelt like I did," Donny replied.

"She was completely bare-ass nekkid?" I asked in disbelief.

"Naked as a jay bird, unless you count the high heels she had on."

"She kept her shoes on? No kidding? What happened next?" I asked.

"She was just starting to spin around a pole on the stage when I was grabbed from behind. A pair of hands latched onto me like a bear trap. Grabbed me by my collar and the back of my belt and dragged me back from under the tent. I swear it was the biggest, meanest carnie in the whole shooting match here. He didn't say a word, just hoisted me around a couple of times like he was getting ready to throw a discus and launched me about twenty feet into a huge mud puddle back there. I hit belly first and skidded through it, rolled up out of it, and kept moving."

"What about that blonde? Was she naked, too?" I wanted to know the important stuff, not the trivial side notes.

"I didn't see the blonde! Didn't you hear me? I got chucked like a Frisbee into a mudhole by a bouncer with arms like a hairy fence post!!"

"How about the brunette? Did you see the brunette?"

"Bite me!" Donny said. "I'm heading to the restrooms to see if I can rinse some of this crud off me. I'll meet you guys in the arcade."

He started off.

"Wait a minute!" I shouted at him. "What color were the shoes?"

He made a hand gesture to me, and I took it to mean that he really didn't care what color the shoes were.

I met Kirk when he came out after the show. He had always talked a good game about his knowledge of the female form. Surely he could fill me in on the activities within the tent.

But I couldn't get diddly-squat out of him. His sophisticated, man-of-the-world façade had been overwhelmed by what he had seen up on the stage of the girlie show that night.

It had been peeled away along with the clothes of the strippers. All that remained was the naive farm boy in him, and it left him behaving as if he now belonged to an exclusive club. He had seen the revered Girlie Bits Garden and would not divulge the secret handshake. Hell, he wouldn't even tell me the color of their shoes.

~

WOODCHUCK WARS

Our family isn't native to Vermont. We didn't move here until 1767. Like most people who live close to the land, we prided ourselves on being self-sufficient and able to take care of our own. We always had a large garden with corn, potatoes, cucumber, squash, onions, radishes, tomatoes, and just about any other vegetable that we could ripen in Vermont's short growing season. Dad used to say we had eight months of winter and four months of late fall.

Because we relied on our garden for a lot of our food, pests were always a concern. When I was old enough to use a gun, one of my duties was to serve up hot lead to any varmint that dared to cross the boundaries of our garden. Sometimes I shot them even before they made it onto that hallowed ground.

A family of skunks or raccoons can ruin a corn patch in a night or two. Gray squirrels and woodchucks are a constant bother to gardeners. Starlings pull up seed corn as fast as it sprouts. We were in a constant battle, and we tried to be on the winning side. Sometimes it was hard to tell the winners from the losers.

One late summer night when I was about fifteen, my dad came in from sitting out on the side deck. He said, "I think there's a 'coon in the corn. I can hear it tearing down the stalks."

He called my dog, Wolfie, a German Wirehaired Pointer, and we went outside. We walked him to the edge of the garden, and Dad and I could hear something in there, tearing it up. So did Wolfie.

"Go get 'im, boy!" my dad shouted.

Wolfie disappeared into the rows of corn, and we soon heard him thrashing and growling after the interloper. Then we heard him whine, and the pungent odor of skunk came wafting to us. Wolfie came running out, stinking to high heaven, blinded and sneezing from the spray he'd gotten. He ran up to my dad and gave a good shake and sneeze and sent a yellow halo of skunk all around him and onto my Old Man. It took quite a few cans of tomato juice and numerous baths until they were back to normal. Dad had to burn his favorite flannel shirt.

The grandest battle of all occurred in the summer of '68 when I was eleven. The Old Man had planted darn near half an acre of garden on the back edge of the yard, down near the railroad fence. About the same time he'd started turning up the sod, the woodchucks had turned up, too. By the end of June, we had the woodchuck equivalent of Ma, Pa, and the kids munching on just about everything growing in the garden. Except the weeds. They didn't touch the weeds. Scarecrows were the first line of defense the Old Man tried.

"Dad," I said, as he nailed up the first one. It was sporting a yellow flowered sundress and an old blue Easter bonnet, "How are scarecrows going to do any good? We're not having any problems with crows."

"Nobody likes a wise ass," he replied. "First off, I'll get the woodchucks scared of people. Then these will work just fine. You have to be smarter than a woodchuck to outfox them."

Apparently, nobody had informed the woodchucks that the Old Man was smarter than they were. He took potshots at them from the tool shed and the back porch with his shotgun. Fortunately for the woodchucks, the garden was just out of effective range. So Dad's efforts to make them scared of people didn't pan out the way he'd hoped. It only served to train them to be scared of people who were on the porch or in the tool shed. They were quite friendly with the fake ones permanently planted in the middle of the garden. They would actually eat in the shade of the scarecrows on hot days.

But to my Old Man, this was war. No rodents were going to deprive us of the food we needed to get us through the winter. I was going to suggest he put on the sundress and Easter bonnet and stand out there with his gun under his skirt. But I knew that would go over like a fart in church. Chances were I'd get the "wise-ass" comment again, if not worse. The application of his foot to my ass was not beyond the realm of possibilities. He'd done it before.

When the woodchucks got tired of being shot at, they became nocturnal. Oh, you might see them briefly at first light or just at dusk. But Mom wouldn't let the Old Man touch off a shot at that time of day. Especially after the time he snapped a shot at one as it was hightailing it across the side lawn for the sanctuary of the gully. He missed the chuck but shot out a window in the barn, which he cleverly used as a backstop, gun safety always being paramount.

"Yes, sir, you need to have a good solid backstop when you're shooting," he said while we were fixing the window in the barn. "You can never be too safe. Let this be a lesson to you, Boy."

The Old Man then resorted to psychological warfare. He hung a radio on a pole in the middle of the family of scarecrows and put a metal sap bucket upside down over it to keep off the rain. Then he ran an extension cord out there and tuned the radio to the local rock-and-roll station.

"If this long-hair hippie music doesn't drive them nuts, I don't know what will," the Old Man said. I couldn't help but agree with this tactic. I had seen the effect the rock- and-roll music had on the Old Man.

Just the previous week my older sisters' incessant playing of "I Can't Get No Satisfaction" by the Rolling Stones had caused Dad to rip the record off the hi-fi and sail it off the side porch out into the cow pasture.

Unfortunately for the Old Man, the music on the radio didn't deter the woodchucks from devouring our garden. Secretly, I was starting to root for them.

Some vegetables weren't real high on my preferred foods list anyway. In my imagination, I could see the furry thieves out in the garden at night. They'd be out between the rows, dancing the twist to Chubby Checker while munching on dreaded eggplant and horseradish. On windy days, it even looked as though the scarecrows were bopping along to the tunes.

In early August, the war escalated. It coincided with our having our septic tank pumped. The Old Man had dug up the old steel cover and had a pump truck come in and pump the tank out. All that remained were some of the worst dregs that he had bailed out of the distribution box into two five gallon buckets. He was lugging them out towards the garden.

"What're you going to do with those?" I asked as I trailed behind at a safe distance from him, trying to stay upwind.

"I'll show you what I'm going to do with them," he said as he approached the entrance to the woodchucks' burrow. He proceeded to dump the contents of the first bucket down the hole.

"This ought to fix their little red wagon," he chuckled as he started to empty the second bucket down the den. His laughter was cut short when a very wet, very smelly, and quite angry woodchuck came shooting out of the hole like a missile coming out of its silo.

The Old Man let out a string of words that were both colorful and new to my limited cussing vocabulary at the time.

As the profanity rolled out of his mouth while back-pedaling away from the hole, trying to avoid the deranged creature advancing on him, the Old Man tripped and fell over backwards, spilling most of the bucket's sewage into his lap. I quickly assessed the situation and wisely retreated to the slide on the swing set nearby. This was not only safer but also afforded a better view of the battle as it unfolded in front of me.

I watched in fascination as my father fought hand-to-paw with a crazed woodchuck that I swear was wearing what looked like a toilet-paper bandanna throughout the entire engagement.

It was the bucket that saved the Old Man. He used it deftly, and with considerable skill, to fend off the wet, angry rodent. He actually landed a few good shots while flailing for his life. They came with a price, though, for as he was swinging the bucket about, he was also spewing the remains of the dreaded contents all over himself.

The woodchuck finally broke off the attack and made a dash for the gully with the Old Man in hot pursuit, yelling for it to come back and finish the fight. He threw his bucket at the varmint as it dove down a secondary den entrance.

"I never heard of a woodchuck attacking a person unprovoked before," he said, as he staggered back from the edge of the gully, panting like a sheepdog in summer.

"Unprovoked?" I said. "You started it."

He turned to glare at me. "Nobody likes a wise ass, Boy."

I could almost see the stench that wafted off him. The wind shifted and not to my favor, so I slid down the slide. "I Can't Get No Satisfaction" came drifting up to us from the radio in the garden. I skedaddled for the house while the getting was good.

~

THE GOLD DUST TWINS

Growing up the youngest of six kids had its advantages and its pitfalls. I don't recall wearing much of anything that wasn't a hand-me-down from a sibling or a cousin. I never owned a new pair of ice skates. And a fella can sure take a ribbing when he shows up to play hockey wearing girl's white figure skates.

Whenever I complained to my Old Man about my lack of anything new, he'd trot out some of the hardships he endured as a kid during the Great Depression.

"You think you've got it tough? We had to eat our cereal with a fork and pass the milk on to the next kid," he'd say.

"I never had a new pair of shoes until I enlisted in the Navy during WWII, The Big One. I'd go barefoot from spring till fall. My feet would get so tough, I'd wrap barbed wire around them just for traction."

We knew he was greening us, but there was no way to dispute his claims.

My Aunt Polly's youngest boy, Donny, was one year older than me, right between George and me. He was their youngest, so I was lucky enough to get his hand-me-downs. He and I were close friends. It was the country mouse and city mouse type of relationship. And that city mouse was always getting this country mouse in hot water.

He was from Winooski, a city that had a rather shady reputation. There was an old joke about a young couple making out in the boy's car. During a heated exchange in the back seat, she tells him to "kiss me where it stinks." He jumps back into the front seat and drives her to Winooski.

Whenever Donny visited, my Old Man would go on red alert. He would come home from his job at the Burlington Rapid Transit Company's bus garage, look us both up and down, and ask, "How much damage did you do today?"

He figured it was a good day if he came home and the barn was still standing and the cops weren't waiting for him.

There was the incident in the spring of '69 that the Old Man referred to as "The Inferno."

By the end of that day he'd lost his eyebrows. But on the plus side, he'd gained a healthy respect for fire safety.

Every spring he would burn the grass in the side pasture to help keep the brush down. He later admitted, under cross-examination, that he should have known better than to leave Donny and me or, as he put it, "two pyromaniacs," alone to tend that grass fire while he went inside to "take a squirt." When he came back out, the fire was skipping its way down through the gully and into the puckerbrush along the sides of the railroad tracks.

I had never seen my Old Man move so fast under his own power before that flame-filled day, and haven't since. He attacked the fire with a well-known Vermont firefighting technique: using the highly regarded broom rake. With the help of his fanning, the Old Man had the flames licking up the sides of the telegraph poles.

During a heated attack on a blazing patch of blackberry bushes, his broom rake snapped in two. For a second, I thought he was in trouble, but he didn't miss a beat. He cast the pieces of his broken weapon aside, ran up to a small pine tree, and tore it up by the roots and continued to flail at the fire with that.

I found the whole inferno quite amusing. The Old Man, less so. He said that if it hadn't been for the train trestle over the river, the inferno would have made it to Richmond, seven miles down the line. He never lit a match outside again for twenty years.

Our neighbor, Garth Perkins, referred to Donny and me as the Gold Dust Twins. We were always covered with dust and dirt from our latest exploits, but that wasn't why he gave us that nickname. No, we earned that golden title because of the clouds of dust we generated racing every motorized apparatus we could lay our hands on.

I was fortunate to have a father who was a first-class mechanic. I don't know how I conned him into being our willing pit crew. He probably had done the math and surmised that it was cheaper and safer to keep us occupied in a known activity than to leave us to our own devices. After all, his eyebrows had taken quite a while to grow back.

My career with motorized wheels started with a mini-bike and a go-cart. The go-cart was a relic my dad had gotten from a fellow gearhead down at the Burlington bus garage. The clutch was shot, and the air breather was missing.

I put my financial resources, which were considerable, up to fund the repairs. I was pulling down fifty cents a week allowance and making ten cents a row weeding the family garden. The rows were just slightly shorter than the outfield at Fenway. I spent my hard-earned wages on a new clutch from the Monkey Wards catalog. The Old Man rigged up an air filter with some metal screening and cheese cloth.

We soon had the go-cart up and running. Well, running anyway. The frame had taken a beating from some lard butt who had literally ridden it into the ground. That go-cart had a swayback that made it look like an over-ridden horse. Its ground clearance was so slight that you couldn't straddle a hen turd without bumping your butt on it. Seat cushion?

Nope. But the wheels would turn, and it would go, and that was all we needed or cared about.

The mini-bike came next and was worse than the go-cart. I had rescued the rusted remains on a Saturday dump run with my dad. A lot of our dump runs were even-Steven as to what we took to the dump and what we brought back from the dump.

The mini-bike's tires were smooth as a toad's belly and it lacked a seat and motor, but to me those were just minor details. The engine that I ended up putting on it was only about a three-and-a- half horsepower. It didn't have a recoil pull start. What it had was a three-foot piece of rope with a little wooden handle on one end and a knot on the other.

To start that engine we took the knot on the end of the rope and slid it behind a notch in a cup- shaped hunk of metal that stuck out on the side of the motor. The cup was fastened to the crank shaft. I'd wrap the rope around the cup until it got down to the wooden handle, and then I'd pull for all I was worth. It'd take a few pulls to get her started. Sometimes the knotted end of the rope would whip off of it and catch me right on the cheek like a bull whip. It damn near put my eye out a couple of times.

The Old Man rigged up a belt and chain reduction gear to the rear axle that would eat a pant leg in a heartbeat. When it got done with the pants, it would start on our skin. If that didn't get us, the cup-shape chunk of metal spinning at twice the speed of light would.

Those things were on the right side of the bike. On the left side was the exhaust muffler. It stuck out by our calf and got up to approximately three thousand degrees. If I was real brave, or stupid, depending on who you asked, I would wear shorts and forgo the pant-leg-eating part of the ride and go right to the skin-eating/leg-burning part.

The only brake on the bike was a pedal that was uncomfortably close to the exhaust muffler. I have places on my leg that are still devoid of hair follicles. The pedal worked a pad that rubbed on the rear tire and might have stopped us if we'd been going about one mile every two weeks. We were better off dragging our feet, using the time-tested Fred Flintstone method of braking. Yabba-dabba-do.

Cousin Donny and I rode those two contraptions over in the sandpit and around the cow pastures. We stopped only when we ran out of gas. And we learned to be experts at siphoning petrol from any fuel tank on the farm. After a mouthful or two of gas, you learned quickly or puked. And nothing was worse than burping gas fumes at supper to alert the Old Man to our gas-snitching ways.

We had to be careful with the mini-bike in the cow pastures. We didn't want to run over fresh cow flops, especially on a hot day. The bike didn't have any fenders, and if we didn't keep our eyes peeled, we would end up speckled with cow turd. We avoided them like land mines but considered them only minor inconveniences.

Late in the summer following the inferno, Donny and I were sitting around by the backside toolshed on an old picnic table. We had a Coleman lantern lit, as it was getting toward dark. It had been a long, dusty day. The Gold Dust Twins were alive and well.

"I can't believe you went over the edge of the sand pit where you did," I said to Donny.

"I can't believe you were stupid enough to follow me!" he replied. He picked up a gas jug with some gas he had just pilfered out of the Old Man's tractor. He walked over to fuel up Old Blister, as we'd come to call the go-cart. It was a calm night and the stars were just peeking out as he tipped the gas can up to fill the tank. I was sitting on the tabletop with my feet on the bench as I watched him pour the gas. There was a sudden "SWOOSH!" as a string of white flame shot from the burning lantern to the gas jug when the fumes drifted over to it.

It looked as if the lantern had briefly turned into a flame thrower. Donny screamed and jumped backwards, spilling gas all over himself. I just sat there with my mouth open as he circled the table, lit up like a torch.

As he began his second pass, the Old Man appeared out of nowhere. He grabbed his flaming nephew and rolled him on the ground until the fire was snuffed out. I finally came to life and ran over and beat out the flames on the go- cart with a sweatshirt. Old Blister had really gotten blistered. Luckily, Donny came out of it with just a few minor burns on his hands. And, of course, he'd lost his eyebrows

~

GOING ONCE, GOING TWICE

When I was growing up, free entertainment wasn't hard
to come by if a kid knew where to look. A trip anywhere was rated as something to do. I was always raring to
go, unless the trip involved the doctor's office or the dentist. I
would horn in on any errand that my dad went on.

Trips to the town dump were well known to produce arti-
facts of cast-off junk from other townsfolk that could keep a
kid like me busy for days. I didn't know it at the time, but I was
on the forefront of the recycling movement.

A beat-up baby carriage could be cannibalized into a
coaster go-cart. Old inner tubes could be just the ticket for
making a water-balloon-launching howitzer that could rain
havoc down on my neighborhood enemies from a good safe
distance. All I had to do was get my hands on the stuff.

My Old Man would quite often try to discourage me from
bringing home some of my poorer choices. But that meant he

might have to give up some of his own selected crap. When we were leaving the dump and he was strapping down a cast-iron bathtub missing two legs into the back of the truck, it was literally child's play for me to sneak a couple of busted-up skateboards in there, too.

These things just needed a little ingenuity to repurpose. The tub became a watering trough for our cows across the road. I pried the skateboard's wheels off and used them for the prototype of my first pair of snowshoe roller skates.

Another surefire bet for a good time was going to an auction. Farm auctions were the best. But any auction would do. There was a monthly auction house up at Cady's Falls called, and I'm not making this up, Hick's Commission Sales. They might not have been selling hicks, but they sure were drawing them in.

The swarm of humanity that came out of the woods and farms each month to go to Hick's auctions was a sight to see. The closest thing I can compare it to would be any Vermont country fair on Demolition Derby Day. Or watching the horde of shoppers at the St. Albans Walmart on the first of the month. From horses to hairpins, it was fascinating to watch the bidding and dickering of the crusty hay-shaker farmers and tobacco-spitting woodchucks as bids ricocheted back and forth between them and the auctioneer.

The auctioneer was customarily a high-spirited joker, wound tighter than a three-day clock. He could sell a bull moose a hat rack and make every bidder feel as though they were getting the deal of a lifetime. And that the deal was about to slip through their fingers unless they made just one more, measly bid.

Most auctioneers also had an assistant who brought out

each object for sale. This collaborator worked with the auctioneer, affirming that the item up for bidding was indeed in mint condition and well maintained. He also helped spot the numerous subtle bidding signals the audience employed to place their bids. These covert gestures could range from a tug on a hat brim, a scratch of an ear, or a minuscule nod of the head. Actually raising your hand up in full view was considered poor form and the sign of a rookie or out-of-stater.

These practices led to my buddy, Kirk Perkins, almost owning a silage wagon at Armand St. Dennis's farm auction. The St. Dennises lived on a farm just east of the Perkins' farm. They had decided to sell out because, as Armand put it, he'd had enough of his cows "eating and shitting him into bankruptcy."

I was fourteen, which meant Kirk was fifteen. Kirk had big bushy sideburns and looked older than he was. We were in the back of the crowd, perched up on a hay wagon that had been sold off. It offered a good view as the crowd moved onto the next item, the silage wagon.

As the bidding commenced on the silage wagon, a hornet lighted on Kirk's hat.

"A hornet just landed on your hat on the side of your head," I said as the bidding hit $300. Kirk was scared stiff of bees of any sort. He lost all interest in the bidding and took a swipe at the side of his head.

"$325 on the hay wagon!" shouted the spotter assistant to the auctioneer. The auctioneer quickly got a $350 bid from a guy wearing a John Deere hat on the far side of the crowd.

"You missed him." I said. "He's still there."

Kirk swatted at the other side of his head and upped his bid to $375. John Deere hat bid $400.

The hornet took offense to being swatted at. It flew off and circled right back and dive-bombed Kirk who took a defensive swing at it and in doing so bid $425. John Deere bid $450.

The hornet broke off the attack. Kirk shook his head back and forth.

"Whew!" he said. "That was close. I almost got stung!"

The auctioneer took Kirk's head shaking to mean he was out of the bidding.

"Going once! Going twice! Sold! To the man in the John Deere hat for $450."

Garth, Kirk's dad, made his way over to us as we climbed down off the hay wagon.

"What the hell you doing, Boy?" He said to Kirk. "We don't need another silage wagon. And if we did, I'd do the bidding. You're goddamned lucky that guy outbid you, or you'd be sleeping in it tonight!"

Kirk looked at his father as though he was daffy. He didn't have a clue that he'd been bidding on anything. Of course, I knew exactly what I'd done. If that hornet had just stuck around, I think Kirk could've gotten that silage wagon for $475.

My Old Man bought St. Dennis's John Deere 14-T hay baler at that auction. This meant we could retire the monster International Harvester baler we'd been using. It dropped bales the size of a boxcar that weighed only slightly less. The John Deere 14-T spit out nice little square bales even I could lift.

My dad didn't sell the old I.H. though. He dismantled it and kept the parts for other projects. Pieces of the old baler showed up in wood splitters and logging arches and numerous other inventions for years.

We acquired some good things and some odd things at auctions. Occasionally, some good odd things.

We went to a farm auction up in the Champlain Islands that netted us one of my dad's strangest purchases. One of my Old Man's friends named Jerry Goodenough accompanied us. He was quite a few years younger than Dad, but they got along well. Jerry was a highly charged, enterprising type of guy who always had more irons in the fire than a village blacksmith.

He was an electrician by trade, which is how Dad met him—Jerry had done some electrical work at the garage where my Dad worked. Jerry had a dump truck and trailer. A bulldozer, backhoe, bucket loader, dragline, and a couple farm tractors, and livestock. He sold hay and firewood, and ran a farm stand. He kept busy.

One of the items at the auction was a forty-foot-tall wooden silo that was along the backside of the barn. Dad and Jerry got to talking about it, and how much good lumber they could get from it. They also discussed how to go about dismantling it and getting it away from the barn without smashing the silo, the barn, or themselves to smithereens.

The auctioneer opened the bidding on the silo at $150. There were no takers. He kept lowering it down in twenty-five-dollar increments. When he hit fifty dollars, my Old Man placed the one and only bid. He said that if he'd waited, he might have gotten it for twenty-five. When we got home, Dad told my mom that he'd bought an old wooden silo for fifty dollars.

She looked at him and said, "A what?"

"A silo," Dad said. "There's lots of good lumber in it once we get it dismantled. It was just too good a deal to pass up."

"Right," she replied. "I'll be remembering that line the next time J.C. Penney has a clearance sale."

The following weekend I went with my dad and Jerry back up to the Islands to get the silo. Jerry brought his dump truck and towed a lowboy trailer. He had a long piece of cable and two big extension ladders, too. I rode with Dad in his pickup loaded with assorted sledgehammers and pry bars.

We were able to attach the cable to a four-by-four inserted crossways inside a small window up in the peak of the silo and hitched it to the trailer hitch on Jerry's dump truck. Then we carefully removed a row of the vertical boards at the bottom of the silo on the side away from the barn, which was the way we planned to pull it. It was sort of like notching a tree in the direction you want it to fall. When we tugged it over, it came down nice and easy, and we broke only a few boards.

The silo turned out to be one of best things Dad ever bought. The boards were three inches thick, tongue-and-groove, and tough as nails because they were made from hemlock. We used them everywhere, and I still have a few of them overhead in the barn today.

The boards from the silo weren't the only thing Dad purchased at an auction that was tough as nails. One deer season when the Old Man and his cronies made a road trip to Hick's Commission Sales, he brought home a big box with assorted ribbon candy and taffy. We kids thought we'd struck gold. Then we tried to eat it. The stuff was probably made during the Coolidge administration. The choice was either to bust a tooth on the ribbon candy or pull some out with the taffy. It was terrible.

Dad ended up giving it to the tribe of kids who lived along the road near the turn leading down to our camp. His hope was that bribery might induce them to keep an eye on the camp for us and guard it from vandals who occasionally caused trouble there. He knew the most likely suspects were among the beneficiaries of his largess. I don't know if he really thought giving them that stale old stuff would help, or if he was just trying to get even.

. . .

The first and only pigs we raised were a couple the Old Man bought at a Hick's auction early one spring. Before that we'd never raised anything but beef cows. One time I asked him why we hadn't ever had pigs or chickens.

"Well, grain's expensive," he said, "and pigs and chickens need grain. Our cows don't know what grain is, and that's the way I'm going to keep it. And once you have grain on a farm, you have rats. I don't want rats. Rats can spread disease."

There was another reason, one he didn't tell me. One I'd find out later.

Dad built a pigpen in a corner downstairs in the barn, where the stalls to feed the cows during the winter were located. Underneath the enclosed stairway going down was the water pump for the barn. Getting water for the pigs involved kneeling down, opening a small door, and pulling out about fifteen feet of hose. Once we'd positioned the hose in the water trough, there was an electrical switch just inside the little door we had to turn on, and then we had to reach way back in to crank the faucet on.

One summer evening early in September, just as the pigs were getting near their finished weight, Dad and I were in the barn feeding and watering the two porkers. He opened the little door and reached in, got the hose out, and gave it to me. I set it in their watering trough. I was standing behind him as he knelt down and flipped the electrical switch, then reached in to turn the faucet on. A rat the size of a woodchuck clambered up his outstretched arm, up over his shoulder, and jumped off his back, headed for the safety of the hay mangers.

There were twelve steps going up out of the lower barn. Dad hit just three of them on his way out, after he'd knocked me out of his way. He was still pale and shaking when I came out a few seconds later.

I'd discovered my Old Man's Kryptonite. Rats. And just as Superman created a shield made of lead to protect himself, my dad improvised his own brand of defense against his furry nemesis. From that day forward, he always made me turn the water on.

~

Yes, I Wood

I was one year old when we moved into the house my dad was building in Essex with help from his friends: plumber friends, carpenter friends, electrician friends. In my dad's world, that's what friends did for each other. Dad was their mechanic friend, and he was always fixing their broken machines.

My family lived in the cellar of that house for three years. All eight of us. In the cellar.

For three freaking years. But every path has some puddles, and when we finally moved upstairs it was as if the heavens had opened and the sun come out.

Now that we weren't all confined in the basement, and he didn't have to worry about kids running around in that cramped space, my dad soon attached a woodstove insert to the fireplace down there.

We had a fireplace upstairs in the living room as well, but we used that more for ambiance than heat. There was hot-water baseboard heat upstairs and radiators in the basement, too, all heated by an oil furnace.

But fuel oil costs money. And, with the right connections, wood is free. Dad's connection was Richard Littlewood, who was developing a parcel of wooded property just a half a mile down the road from us. Richard needed roads and building lots cleared of the trees. In exchange for clearing those trees out of the way, Dad got the wood. It was mostly red oak, beech, and maple. Darn good firewood.

Now when I say free wood, that doesn't mean it didn't cost us anything. My dad bought a brand new McCulloch 1-42 chainsaw. In 1962, it was on the cutting edge of chainsaw technology. Meaning that it could beat a crosscut saw. Not by a whole lot, but beat it. Then he also bought axes and splitting mauls, along with numerous replacement handles. Pulp hooks and peaveys. And, despite planting numerous steel splitting wedges in the woods, we never got a single one to grow. So we had to replace those.

After the cost of bandages and blisters was factored in, along with the price of a hernia operation, we could've burned fuel oil with the thermostat set at eighty and came out in better shape. But I'm thankful my Old Man didn't see it that way. Because I loved being out in the woods with him. Watching him fell a tree and turn it into fuel to keep us all toasty and warm during the long, cold winters was something that connected me to the land and showed me what responsibility truly was.

My Old Man supplied not only our house with firewood, but also his parents'. They had a small farm in Hinesburg, and their sole heat source was wood. They used it to run their kitchen and living room stoves eight months of the year.

From an early age I helped stack wood at home and in my grandparents' woodshed, which was approximately the size of a gymnasium. Every year my dad would recruit some of the same friends who had helped build our house to aid him in his effort to fill that cavernous shed. One of his best friends was Joe Flint. Joe drove buses for Burlington Rapid Transit, the same company my Old Man worked for. Joe had a shiftless older brother named Lafe. Dad would hire Lafe to haul the wood in his dump truck.

Joe was a hard worker and would give you the shirt off his back. Lafe was not of the same mold. He would take the shirt and sell it to the highest bidder.

Lafe was always spreading himself too thin, making commitments he couldn't keep. He made money wheeling and dealing in the farming and construction trade. Just getting him to show up was an accomplishment. But when he did show up, he was going full bore. What my dad called "bulling and jamming."

Throwing eighteen-inch-long split firewood up into the back of a seven-yard dump truck is not an easy task when you're a scrawny kid. I was the second smallest kid in my class all through grammar school. But I'd heave the wood up into the truck as best I could. Once the truck got close to full, it was even harder to get pieces of wood up on top. I'd take my time and pick my spots to land them on the load.

One September Saturday, Joe and I were loading the truck. Lafe came over to us and said, "Let me show you how it's done, boys." He started throwing wood up into his truck like a wild man. He was hardly looking at where the pieces were landing. I kept pecking away at the slow, steady pace I was going.

After about five minutes of chucking wood like crazy, Lafe was starting to run out of moxie. He threw a chunk up near the headboard, and it bounced off it and took a hop up over the side and smashed the passenger side mirror on his truck into tiny pieces.

"Well if that don't take the roof off the barn!" Lafe walked over and looked at the broken mirror. "I wish you'd be more careful throwing wood into my truck," he said to me. "That will have to come out of your pay."

"Good luck with that. I ain't getting any pay. Besides, I didn't throw that piece of wood. You did," I informed him.

"So I just busted the mirror off of my own truck? Now why would I do that?" "Dogged if I know," I replied. "But it wasn't me."

"I can vouch for that," said Joe. "If you'd watched where you were throwing, you'd of seen it, too."

Lafe came back to the woodpile and began right where he'd left off, heaving wood up into the truck like he was mad at it, because now he was pissed off about breaking his mirror. And when he bounced another chunk of firewood over the other sideboard and smashed his driver's side mirror, I thought he was going to blow a gasket.

"Well, shit fire and save the matches!" he yelled. "Another one of my mirrors shot to hell!"

"You're two for two on the side mirrors," said Joe. "Maybe you can bounce one over the top and break the windshield."

I found an old shirt behind the seat of my dad's pickup and used it to bundle up all the broken glass on the ground from the mirrors. It was obvious Lafe wasn't going to bother with it.

When the truck was finally loaded, Lafe jumped behind the wheel with Joe riding shotgun, and lit out of there like a big ass bird and headed for my grandparents' farm. My dad and I followed behind in his pickup, freighted to the gills with a load of the shorter, smaller- diameter kitchen wood.

"Lafe broke both his side mirrors. How's he going to see behind him?" I asked.

"I don't think Lafe spends a whole lot of time looking back," answered the Old Man. "And it's just as well. Something might be gaining on him."

My grandparents' farm could've been pulled right out of the 1940s. Grandpa still put loose hay up in the barn. Always kept a milk cow or two, along with a steer for beef. There were chickens in the yard and ducks and geese on the little farm pond out back where I could catch bullhead. And there was always a hog or two to be found rooting about the barnyard. Their vegetable garden was one of the best kept I'd ever seen, with the widest variety of plants you could think of. They had a raspberry and strawberry patch to boot.

Diversity wasn't a catchphrase like it is now. It was a way of life for the old couple and served them well. Sure, they were tied down to the farm, but they didn't have any other place they'd rather be.

The best part about filling their woodshed was the meals that Grandma would make for the crew that was helping to get their wood in. She was a top notch cook and knew how to put on a spread. Thank God, because the quantity of vittles Dad's friends could eat was beyond belief.

One of them, Fred Mazoot, was a big guy. He sat next to me at the table on this one occasion. A rack of a dozen warm homemade rolls was in front of him. Grandma's rolls would melt in your mouth, right along with the fresh butter she churned. Fred broke off four rolls, put them back, and kept eight.

But it was the desserts that always had my full attention. I'd try not to bloat up on the main meal so I'd have room for them. Sheet cake with chocolate frosting thick as fudge. Apple and berry pies with fresh whipped cream and slices of sharp cheddar. All kinds of cookies that made your mouth water. And fresh milk, straight from the teat and ice cold from the fridge to wash it all down.

At the end of the day we were all gathered around the back of the woodshed by the vehicles. Lafe was picking out a few pieces of glass that still clung to the frame of his truck's mirrors. Everybody was shooting the breeze a bit before packing up to head home. We were full of good food and good cheer, content with the fact that we had all come together and gotten the job done. My Old Man decided this would be a good time to settle up with Lafe for the use of his truck.

"Here you go, Lafe. Twenty dollars a load like we agreed," Dad said as he handed him forty dollars for the two loads Lafe had hauled that day.

Lafe took the wad of ones and fives from my dad that Grandma had given him from her egg money.

"What about my two broke mirrors? They'll cost me at least ten dollars apiece to replace."

"You broke those," Joe piped up. "You should pay for them yourself."

"No," said my dad as he took a twenty-dollar bill out of his wallet and handed it to Lafe. "He wouldn't have busted them if he hadn't been throwing in wood for me."

"That's right," said Lafe. He took the money from my dad and tucked it in his pocket.

We all said our so longs, and I got into the pickup with my Old Man.

"You did a good day's work, Son. Thanks for the help," Dad said as we drove home. "I'll put a little extra in your allowance next week."

"Thanks," I said. "I'm getting low on .22 shells. Boy, grandma sure can cook. Did you always eat like that when you were a kid?"

"Well, we never had much money. Most people didn't. And sometimes we were living on high hopes. But we always had enough to eat. And we always shared what we had when we could. Even during The Depression, ma would find something to feed the hobos that rode the trains near our farm who would stop by looking for a handout."

We drove along in silence for a while as I watched the familiar landscape of the rugged green hills go by. Finally, I had to ask.

"Why did you give Lafe the money for busting his mirrors? He broke them bulling and jamming the way he does. He should've paid for them himself."

"You're right, he did break those mirrors. But Lafe doesn't see it that way. He always looks for somebody else to blame. You'll find some people can't accept responsibility for what they do. Can't admit that they're wrong. Guys like Lafe think everything should work out in their favor. But life isn't like that, and they end up spending their time always pissed off at something or somebody."

We pulled up to a stop sign at Route 2. He turned and looked at me.

"What would I have gained by arguing with Lafe about those mirrors? I'm sure I wouldn't have changed his mind about it one bit. All I would've done was put an unpleasant end to a pleasant day and a good deed done by us for my folks. Sometimes it's better to be happy than it is to be right. You'll find life's a lot easier when you plow around the stumps."

As I took in what he'd said, we crossed Route 2 and went onto North Williston Road, on our way to the home he and his friends had built for us with their own two hands.

What I had first seen as weakness in my Old Man when he gladly handed over that twenty dollars to Lafe Flint turned out to be one of the greatest strengths a person can have. I'd remember his words and use them for the rest of my life.

MOUNDS OF TROUBLE

It wasn't until I was around eight years old that girls regis-
tered as something more than an aggravation. During third
grade this awareness manifested itself in the time- honored
tradition of chasing my female classmates around various sections of the schoolyard during recess.

Sometimes I was trying to drive them out of an area
claimed as male territory. Of course, we guys made the claim
solely so we could run after the girls and not look like the complete idiots we were.

A few boys were ahead of the game and actually acknowl-
edged that they liked a certain girl. These enlightened individuals were freed from the chasing portion of the ritual. They
were allowed to move on to the more intricate level of inter-
action, which consisted of eye contact, passing notes through
a third party, and, if they were really smitten, maybe sitting at

the same table during lunch with appropriate body buffers between them and the chosen girl.

It was entirely possible to have a relationship blossom, ripen to maturity, and wither on the vine without anything that could pass as a conversation ever taking place. All of this could transpire within a few days. Because, similar to dog years, when a girl is involved, an eight-year-old boy can find one day is equal to roughly two months.

As I struggled up the romantic ladder of learning, I found myself in fifth grade with a better understanding of how to avoid the awkwardness that arises when talking to a girl in person. I stumbled onto a surefire way to hide the sweaty palms, the glazed-over eyeballs, the fear-induced facial tic and/or flatulence that have plagued young romantic recruits for centuries: Call her on the phone.

At first blush, this seemed easy. When I put it into practice, it turned into a time-consuming affair. The preparatory dialog I had to write out ahead of time was more complex than the Treaty of Versailles.

I had to hammer out point and counterpoint opinions on certain topics and have witty repartee ready. I boned up on my knowledge of commonplace subjects as if studying for a midterm exam.

And then there was the emergency exit strategy I had to memorize. Everything from the casual "I have to go let my dog out" to the urgent "I think I smell smoke." The ordeal of placing a simple telephone call could leave a guy too frazzled to pick up the receiver.

When it came to finally dialing the phone number, it could take longer than sending a message by Pony Express. I'd have to go through numerous dry runs. I commonly practiced dialing while holding down the receiver button. This was the era of the rotary telephone. The last digit could be cranked over and held for eternity. Which is how long it could take for some courage to find its way down to the end of a young boy's index finger and let him release the dial, completing the connection.

Seventh grade consisted of a learning curve that had more twists and turns and ups and downs than a roller coaster. I'm not talking about academics. In that category, I was an honor roll student. But when dealing with girls, I didn't know come hither from go yonder.

It was during this period that I started "feeling out" possible physical relationships with certain members of the female sex. I discovered girls are loaded with many pitfalls, snares, and actual booby traps.

Hardstick Elementary ran an after-school program during the winter months, and it offered the seventh- and eighth-grade students the opportunity to go night skiing under the lights at Bolton Valley Ski Resort. For the paltry price of three dollars, a student could attempt to maneuver down the snow-covered slopes of Bolton Mountain.

We guys would also attempt other maneuvers while going up the mountain with our girlfriends on the chairlift, as well as the during the ride home in the dark confines of the school bus.

In fact, for many of us boys, skiing took a backseat to the backseat activities on the bus. We used terms such as "necking" and "making out" to polish the rough edges off the spit- swapping, tongue-wrestling goings-on during the forty-five-minute ride back to the school.

Only the more courageous boys among us had the pluck to attempt the more risky activity of placing a hand on the chest of his female counterpart. That was like a tightrope walker working without a net.

For some, just finding the whereabouts of the sought-after prize was challenging. Considering that our quarry was hidden under several layers of winter apparel, as well as being of limited size, topped off with the lack of any lighting to guide us, this was a hit- or-miss proposition.

But just going on the hunt and being in the vicinity of the prey was heartening enough for me. However, Mary Lovejoy, the girl I was going out with, was a "properly raised young lady." She revoked my hunting privileges on my first sally into the woods. I thought she'd cracked one of my ribs with her pointy little elbow.

I figured it was just a case of bad beginner's luck for me. Sometimes you eat the bear; sometimes the bear eats you. I felt that if I leaned into the harness and kept greasing the skids, sooner of later I'd arrive at my destination.

Eighth grade looked to shape up as a banner year. The town had decided to build a new middle school for grades five through eight, and we would be the first graduating class. After being stuffed into crowded classrooms, church basements, and temporary trailers over the last few years, it was great to be the top dogs in a brand new building. We took to the new school like cold pigs to warm mud.

The after-school skiing program was starting up again that winter. Lip balm and Chapstick would be needed. One of my friends and classmates, Mitch Barker, lived in the Pinewood Manor housing development just down the road from me. Mitch fancied himself as quite a skier. And he was, until he crashed into some trees and rocks and broke both of his legs.

Once he got out of the hospital and was on the mend, his family wanted to keep going on their weekend skiing trips. Mitch being in a wheelchair posed a problem for the rest of the clan.

They solved their dilemma by hiring a friend to stay home with him on those ski days. The worst thing that ever happened to Mitch, that accident, turned out to be a lucrative and enjoyable experience for me.

Mary Lovejoy lived next door to Mitch. Beth Goodhouse lived in Pinewood, too, and was friends with Mary. Beth was going out with Mitch. It wasn't rocket surgery for the four of us to devise ways for the girls to sneak over and visit Mitch and me for hours at a time.

Mitch's parents would supply us with unlimited food and drink, chips and snacks. We two couples would separate into our chosen private area of the Barkers' comfortable new home and surface periodically for air, food, and beverage.

In reality, the girls' virtue was never in the least bit threatened. Since Mitch was in a wheelchair with two legs in casts, his options were limited. Mary made it clear that I would end up with something in a cast if I tried anything south of the equator. And she was very skilled at deflecting my feeble attempts up in her northern hemisphere. I considered the remittance the Barkers gave me combat pay.

Alas, spring finally came. The snow melted off the ski trails, and Mitch shed his casts and walked away from his wheelchair with lips well-puckered in the art of sucking face. And I happily jumped off the Girl Groping Gravy Train that I had ridden all winter and never looked back. I knew many more obstacles in the girlfriend mine field lay hidden ahead of me. Like learning how to dance and not look like I was having a seizure. Seventh- and eighth-grade school dances at the new middle school were social events not to be missed. Now we had a cafeteria to host them in rather than the cavernous echo chamber of a gymnasium at our old school.

As the last school dance of the year approached, we boys were trying to devise some way to "cop a feel" while under the hawk-like eyes of our spiteful principal, Mr. Willphear. The man was meaner than a tied up wolf.

Standing around in the boy's locker room after gym class, a few of us discussed strategy.

"We've got to figure out a way to get the lights dimmed during a slow dance. I bet a fella could snake a hand around into the grill works during a good long slow dance," said Randy St. Amore.

I thought if Randy wanted a chance with a girl, the lights would have to be turned completely off. The whole St. Amore family looked like their idea of dentistry was to line them up and have a goat kick them in the mouth.

"Heck, Randy," I said. "Maybe you can find a girl with a set of knockers on her back. That'd make things a whole lot easier. I bet her dance card would be filled right up, though. Well, at least for the slow ones. But maybe you're onto something with that slow dance idea. All we have to do is make sure the last dance is a long, slow song. Art, you're the president of the Student Council. Can't you rig it so the last dance is a long slow one?"

Art Babcock had been my best friend since third grade. Both students and faculty liked him, and he was smarter than your average bear. If anybody could get a long, slow song onto the record player, Art could.

Over the days leading up to the dance, we finalized our plans. We agreed that the Beatles' "Hey Jude" would be the song that Art would try to get onto the turntable.

Clocking in at seven minutes, eleven seconds, that song should afford ample time for guys to screw up their courage to whatever degree necessary. Or at least to enjoy a good grapple with their girls for a spell.

Our standard practice for slow dancing at the time was for the girl to have both her hands on the guy's shoulders and the boy to have both of his paws on her hips. Couples would then shuffle and rock back and forth to the music while moving about six inches to one side or the other.

The night of the dance arrived, and the evening began with the opposing forces arrayed in the standard defensive positions, boys on one side of the cafeteria, girls on the other. Once the music started, we guys sent small probing forays across to test the waters.

The Sadie Hawkins dance, when the girls ask the boys to dance, was a courage-building success. Even Randy St. Amore got asked to dance, by Wawa Fleetfoot. Wawa was the kind of girl who loved nature in spite of what it had done to her. They were a perfect match.

The first hint of trouble came when a slow dance started to play about halfway through the evening. As the Beatles' song "Yesterday" drifted through the air, couples started to muckle onto each other and sway back and forth.

Despite what the lyrics said, love was not such an easy game to play. Mr. Willphere, the meanest principal to ever stride the halls of Hardstick Elementary, decided things were getting too close for his comfort. Mr. Willphere had been running the school for years like his own private penitentiary with kids serving an eight year sentence. He started going around to couples and prying them apart like a referee in a boxing match when the two opponents have been in the clinch for too long.

The dance was to end at nine o'clock. At ten minutes to nine, Art made his move. Nancy Pringle, the treasurer of the Student Council, was in charge of putting records on the turntable. Art went up and talked to her as he sifted through the records, fishing out "Hey Jude" and handing it to her.

When Three Dog Night's "Joy To The World" finished telling us that Jeremiah was indeed a bullfrog, she put "Hey Jude" on. Walter Pelkey, another conspirator, slid over to the light switches and shut off all but the exit lights as everybody paired up and went into slow dance mode.

When the song hit the second stanza of "Hey Jude" and sang out "don't be afraid, go out and get her," by God, we were ready to do just that. And then it happened. The song ended with a loud scraatch! as Mr. Willphere ripped it off the record player and a parent chaperon turned the lights back on. Then the worst song that we guys could have ever conceived started to play.

"Sugar, Sugar" by the Archies. A pop bubblegum song by a fictitious band made up of a bunch of studio musicians for a Saturday morning cartoon show.

All our high hopes came crashing down. As the syrupy strains of "Sugar, Sugar" rang through the crowded cafeteria, we knew that we had but one choice if we wanted to stay in the good graces of our girlfriends.

We all joined the conga line that had formed, led by Mr. Willphere himself, as it jostled around the perimeter of our dance hall. And I realized, as the lyrics belted out "I'm going to make your life so sweet," that Willphere had us all, as he always did, dancing to his tune.

UNDER ROADS

Vermont's not called the Green Mountain State for nothing. If a person was to iron its peaks and valleys out
flat, it would probably be the size of Texas. There were hills
and ravines all around the home where I was raised, many of
which figured prominently in my outdoor activities. There
was one ravine to the left side of our house that began as a
ditch up by Route 117. It carried rain and snow-melt runoff
that flowed through a two- foot-wide culvert running under
the road. Unless we got a real frog-choker of a rain, there was
never much water running through the culvert except during
the springtime. Other things went through it once in a while.
One such thing being me.

Our neighbors across the road, the Yandows, had a son,
Craiger, who was close to my age. I would go over and play
with him quite often. Until I was eight, I wasn't allowed to
cross Route 117 unless somebody older watched me go across.

One summer afternoon when I was seven, I saw Craiger out playing. He had a newly purchased airplane glider that he was flying around the front yard.

There wasn't anybody handy to see me across the road. So I came up with my own solution: I would go under it. I scooted through the two-foot-wide culvert quite easily. I had to brush off a considerable coating of cobwebs when I emerged from the far end, but that was a small price to pay to horn in on Craiger's new toy. Not to mention it was fun as all get-out to go through the culvert all on my own.

An hour or so later, I heard my mother calling my name, and I knew I'd best beat it for home, try to sneak back without her seeing where I was coming from. Since Yandow's front yard was right adjacent to the ditch the culvert drained, I hunched down below its banks and headed for it like a woodchuck going for it's burrow.

As I popped out like a prairie dog on the other side, a huge, muscular hand immediately grabbed me by the back of my shirt collar and hoisted me off the ground. My dad was astraddle of the culvert, waiting for me. My feet did about sixty miles an hour in midair. If he'd have set me down, those feet would have roto-tilled a furrow you could have planted a row of corn in.

"We told you not to go over there unless somebody watched you cross the road!" he yelled at me as I stopped my twirling legs and braced for what I knew was coming. He gave me a damn good slap on the ass and I trotted off towards the house.

"I didn't go over there," I said over my shoulder. "I went under there."

You would think that I'd have learned my lesson about culverts as the burned hand teaches best, or in this case, the slapped ass. But sometimes one dose of medicine isn't enough to cure the patient. A second spoonful is needed.

In 1970, Dad purchased twenty-two acres of land adjacent to the half acre our camp was on. The property had an old house and barn on it too. It also had a chain of beaver ponds. Dad decided he would put a road right across a beaver dam where the ponds narrowed as they progressed down a ravine with a small brook in it. This would make it possible to access a fair chunk of the property across the ravine.

It would be a major excavation that required a large culvert to take the water under the new road. So Dad hired his friend, Jerry Goodenough, to come up with his back hoe and bulldozer. Jerry was a fairly happy-go-lucky guy, and even though I was only fourteen, he let me drive his bulldozer every now and then when some easy dirt pushing was needed to make the road. It gave me my first good taste of running a piece of heavy equipment.

The ravine that the chain of beaver ponds were in was quite deep. Because of this, we needed to raise the roadbed about ten feet. This required a lot of fill over the three-foot-diameter culvert that dad had designed out of old boiler tanks that he'd strapped together.

The more fill piled on top of a culvert, the longer it needed to be. So this culvert had to be about thirty-five feet long. We laid it almost level, with just a slight downhill run in it to take the water through. So it turned out that thirty-five feet down the ravine, where it emptied out, the culvert was a good seven feet up in the air. Dad filled that spillway pool where the water would hit with a bunch of riprap, large chunks of rock, to cut down on erosion.

In late April after the summer we'd installed the road, my dad and I went up to camp one Saturday so he could cut some firewood and I could to do a little trout fishing. We soon found that there was a serious problem with the culvert. Apparently, the beavers had taken offense at the Old Man building a road on top of their dam and decided to make the best of it by plugging up the culvert and using our new road as their dam.

"Holy moly," I said as we stood on the road looking at the mass of mud and sticks packed around the culvert almost to the top and the pond backed up behind it. "How are we going to get at that so we can unplug it?"

"Those furry bastards," Dad said. "I'll fix their ass. I'll go up to the barn and get a potato hook and we'll dig that crap out of there. It's a good thing you brought your hip boots for fishing. You're going to need 'em." He tossed my hip boots out of the back of the truck, hopped in, and drove off to the barn.

I took my shoes off and put my hip boots on and went down the bank to the side of the culvert and surveyed the situation. I waded towards the end of the culvert and realized that my boots wouldn't be high enough. The water was too deep. I didn't see how we were going to get at the tangle of limbs and sticks, even with a potato hook.

Then I got an inspiration. What if a guy could get at that mess by getting into the culvert's other end, crawling through it, and pulling it apart from in there? I waited a few minutes for Dad to come back so I could run it by him, but he didn't show. I didn't know that a local yokel, Windy Mallard, had stopped by the barn and was shooting the breeze with Dad as only a man named Windy could.

Patience not being my strong suit, I slid down the bank of our road on the lower side and got on top of the culvert where it stuck out a few feet. A small stream of water splashed out of it onto the riprap seven feet below. I got down on my hands and knees on top of the pipe, facing the road, with my feet hung over the culvert's opening. I backed my way off the culvert until I could bend at the waist and get my feet down onto the lower lip. I gripped the edge and lowered myself into it.

It was cold and damp inside the culvert as I looked through it at my destination thirty-five feet ahead. A glimmer of light shone through the other end of the tunnel. I took a few deep breaths to get my gumption up and headed towards the light. I was not, by no means, headed towards my salvation. Not by a long shot. Since I was a fairly short fourteen-year-old, I could hunch down and sort of duck-walk my way forward.

Snow runoff was still coming from the mountains and the water was ice cold as I began to peck away at the mass of sticks packed with mud. I'd been at it for about five minutes when I heard my dad.

"Where the hell are you!?" he called out. "Where'd you go?"

"I'm in here!" I hollered back.

"Get the hell out of there!" he said.

"But I think I can get it unplugged easier from in here!" I shouted back to him. "I think I've almost got it!"

I had made some progress and had removed a considerable amount of debris from the plug, but it was still holding fast. There was a long three-inch-diameter limb all the way across the open end of the culvert that looked to be the main culprit holding up the works. A beaver had chewed it three quarters of the way through right in the middle. I grabbed onto it with both hands, right at the chewed spot, and gave it all I had to pulling it toward me. It bowed in a little but held. I braced my feet better in front of me as I squatted there and tried again.

It broke with a sharp crack and I went ass over tea kettle until my feet hit on the top of the culvert. I got a good cold soaking down my neck and back and right down the crack of my ass that took my breath away. As I sat back upright in the water, there was a loud gushing sound as the whole mass of limbs, sticks, rocks, and mud that had been packed all around the culvert by a herd of hairy engineers started gushing towards me. It was like the stopper had been pulled, and I was in the drain. I screamed, "Holy Shit!" and then I was scrambling for my life.

I rolled over and got on my hands and knees and started pawing myself out of there like a bear running downhill. Considering that I still had my hip boots on, I made pretty good time. Then a sudden thought occurred to me: what am I going to do when I get to the end of this thing? There's a seven-foot drop onto jagged rocks!

As my head and shoulders broke into the daylight, and I looked down at the rock- filled pool to try and pick a spot, a mighty hand reached down from above and grabbed me by the back of my collar. It yanked me out of the culvert like I was a wild nose hair and tossed me over to the grassy bank just as a cascade of water and debris came roaring full bore out of the end of the culvert.

I lay there on my belly in the sweet soft grass, gasping for breath and soaked to the bone by freezing, muddy water. I rolled over onto my back and looked up to see my dad smiling as he sat astraddle the culvert. The bright spring sunshine was glowing behind him like the halo on a guardian angel.

"You're welcome," he said. "Don't let it happen again."

~

Saw It Right Off

I'm sure there are kids who know from the time they're very young what they want to be when they grow up. For whatever reason, they decide they want to be a specific rodent in the rat race of the working world. Parents influence many of these choices.

I was turned down my career path by my Old Man, but not in the way that he hoped. I knew I didn't want to do anything that resembled his job. He worked for the same company for forty-three years. He started at the bottom of the ladder when he was eighteen as a simple, rookie mechanic working on buses. He worked his way up to night foreman, then shop foreman, and finally to superintendent of maintenance.

And from what I could tell, he hated his job a fair amount of the time. Maybe because he couldn't bitch about it at work, he bitched about it at home. But I decided that if I was going to spend forty hours a week doing something, I wanted to enjoy it most of the time. I wanted to work outside. Specifically, in the woods.

It was my Old Man's doing that I enjoyed the smell of fresh sawdust and the satisfaction of splitting a straight-grained block of firewood. It was he who showed me that physical labor is not something to be avoided or be ashamed of. I obtained a deep fulfillment seeing the fruits of my labors piled up before me, whether it was firewood, hay bales, or wilting weeds laid in a row between the growing stalks of corn. I learned my own power. Seeing my achievements was one of the greatest rewards this growing kid could experience.

So much so that when I was sixteen years old, I talked my parents into letting me buy a chainsaw. In 1973, McCulloch chainsaws were the bee's knees of the wood-cutting world. I picked out a Pro Mac-55 with a 16-inch cutting bar. My mother floated me the $250 needed to buy the saw and set up a monthly payment plan.

I felt I could easily meet the payments since I could make scads of money in the timber market I would soon have cornered. By my reasoning, money did grow on trees. I never factored the reality, that I was so green you could have stuck me in the ground and I would have grown, into my financial figuring. What I lacked in experience, I would make up for with enthusiasm.

My safety training with the chainsaw was brief and to the point. My Old Man told me to be careful. Off to the pile of logs I swaggered with my chainsaw in my hand and dollar signs in my head. Dad had brought a few loads of log-length firewood home from the Pinewood Manor housing development where he was clearing the roads and house lots while he was resting from his real job.

He made a deal with me to cut and split the wood. If I did the wood for our house, I could sell what was left. We figured we had twice as much wood as we needed ourselves. So it worked out I did it on halves. Half for him, half for me. And then there was the half-assed way I went about it. I found out quickly that a chainsaw doesn't do you a whole lot of good if it isn't sharp. Dirt and mud on a log can take the edge off the chain. In just two or three cuts it can be duller than a two-year-old hoe and cut wood almost as fast.

I had to learn how to sharpen my chain with a file, and that wasn't the breeze I'd thought it'd be. It took patience, practice, and experience. Things that were in short supply for a teenage boy. But I gnawed through the pile of logs like a beaver with a toothache and was able to make my payments on the loan. Just barely.

It wasn't the quick, easy money I'd thought it would be, but I knew I could earn more money. I just needed to go to the source. I figured if I cut down my own trees and got into actual logging, cut out the middleman, I could easily be the next lumber baron of the state of Vermont and wind up with more money than a pig has grunts.

But one guy couldn't do it alone. I needed help for such a large undertaking. I recruited my best buddy, Art Babcock, into the cause.

Art was smart, loyal, and a hard worker. More important, he had a connection through his church with the Chittenden County forester, Ray Russell. It was damn close to divine intervention that got us our first log job. Our woods career began on a wing and a prayer.

Art and I met with Mr. Russell in his county office and told him of our desire to work in the woods. All we needed was the chance to prove ourselves and we would be on the path to fame and fortune in the timber-harvesting industry. Mr. Russell was at first hesitant to cut us loose on any landowner's property. But we were so determined, I think he figured he could cure us of logging fever with the proper selection of a woodlot.

He brought us to an overgrown cow pasture of white pine in Williston that was the sorriest excuse for a log job in the tri-state area. Trees were growing thicker than the hair on a boar's ass. Limbs started about six inches off the ground and went all the way to the tippity top. Scattered throughout the stand were trees to cut, marked with yellow paint.

There's a bug called the white pine weevil that eats the top terminal bud of young pine trees and this wood lot had been the all-you-can-eat buffet for them. Every time they ate the top bud off, it put another crook in the stem of the tree. The few trees that were big enough for logs were crooked as a pig's pecker. This made the trees marketable only as four-foot pulp and worth a paltry thirteen dollars per cord stacked roadside.

Also marked to cut among the thicket of pines were some huge old pasture pines that were the seed trees for the younger crooked pecker poles. These monsters were about four foot on the stump with massive limbs shooting out in all directions starting a few feet from the ground. Once again, all pulp.

Mr. Russell told us there was a twenty-four-inch maximum diameter limit on pulp, so some of those butt pieces were too big. We'd have to split the four-foot bolts by hand with wedges and a maul to meet the twenty-four-inch limit. He also said that the landowner got three dollars per cord out of the thirteen dollars for the pulp. To top it off, the job had to done in the winter, as there were some wet spots that would have to be frozen for the lot to be workable. We figured we'd best take the job before it got too lucrative and somebody else snatched it up.

It took Art and me some serious groveling and begging, but Art's Dad, Ed, reluctantly volunteered his 9N Ford Jubilee tractor as our means of skidding, as well as his time as operator. Mostly because he didn't trust us alone with his prized tractor. When winter blew in, we'd work the job weekends and during school vacations. Ed eventually taught Art how to drive the tractor, so he could beg off. We preferred that he was gone anyway, because it left us to our own methods of logging. Our primary method being bulling and jamming. Ed was so safety conscious we felt it was cutting into our daily production.

There was one practice Ed frowned on that Art and I found quite entertaining. The big monster pasture trees had numerous big limbs on them and were surrounded by lots of other pine trees. When I cut them, they wouldn't fall to the ground. They would just sort of lean over and get hung up on other trees. The old Jubilee didn't have enough nut in her to pull the behemoths down off the stump.

I discovered that I could work my way up the leaning tree by walking on it and cutting the limbs off as I went. The fun part came when I would cut a limb off that was holding the tree up. The tree would drop down and usually roll one way or the other. Sometimes just a few feet. Sometimes all the way to the ground. And if I was up in it quite a ways and I cut the kingpin that was holding it lodged to another tree, yahoo!, I had to cling to it and stay to the upper side, all while holding my running chainsaw. I would perform a fair imitation of a 148-pound squirrel.

Somehow we survived the winter and came out of it with a clearer understanding of the timber-harvesting trade. One would think that poverty would be a powerful enticement for leaving the woods on the run. For us, it wasn't. I still loved working in the woods. And now felling trees had caught my interest like nothing else before. I knew there had to be a way to make some money doing it, and I decided I'd keep at it until I found one. Plus, I had a chainsaw to pay for.

During the summer I helped clear a building lot and powerline right-of-way for a neighbor. This honed my meager felling skills, as well as my ability to sharpen my chainsaw teeth to a reasonable edge. But in my senior year of high school, I started my logging career in earnest.

I had earned enough class credits in three and a half years of high school that, when the last semester started, the few classes I had were all in the morning. This left the afternoons open for gainful employment. Employment I found working for a logger named Kenny Cutright.

Kenny agreed to pay me $2.50 per hour to cut and limb out trees for him. To receive that top dollar wage I had to supply my own chainsaw, gas, and bar oil. That way Kenny could hire me as a subcontractor and avoid paying for any liability and workmen's' compensation insurance. He pointed out that I probably wouldn't need it anyway.

The winter was brutal that year. Snow right up to the belly button of a nine-foot Indian and colder than a witch's elbow. By the end of the first week working for Kenny, I'd been frozen so much I was farting snowflakes. Running a chainsaw shakes the blood right out of the hands, and they freeze near solid. Luckily, they were frozen to my saw handles and I could keep working.

It was my second week on the job when I was starting to think I was pretty slick with a chainsaw. I had felled a large hemlock tree across a ravine that was about thirty feet across and fifteen feet deep. The butt of the tree rested on one bank, the top on the other bank.

Once a tree is down, the limbs must be trimmed off, so I started to do that. I began walking out on the tree and cutting the limbs off as I went. Pretty soon I was halfway out on the tree with a considerable gap underneath me to the bottom of the ravine. I tried not to think about it and kept cutting off limbs.

Unknown to me, when I had dropped the hemlock across the ravine, I had created what is known as a spring pole. The falling tree had bent over a small sapling underneath it and held it under intense pressure. As I bent over and reached underneath the tree to cut a limb, I inadvertently cut the spring pole. It is aptly named.

It shot out from underneath the hemlock like the arm of a catapult and hit me square in the jaw. It blew my pilot light right out and chucked me and my saw off the tree and down into the ravine. And that's where Kenny found me, led by the sound of my chainsaw still idling beside me in the snow.

When I came to, he helped me up and out of the ravine and sat me on a stump while my head cleared.

"Maybe you ought to head out for the day," he said as he brushed some of the snow off my back. "I've flushed goldfish that look perkier than you."

I sat there and made sure my jaw was still working. I figured Kenny was wondering what sort of a logger he'd hired. And at that minute, so was I. Once I thought about it, though, I knew what I had to do.

"Well Kenny," I said, "if it's all the same to you, I'd rather stay and work my way out of it." And by God I did. I finished out the day. I worked for Kenny straight through until spring break-up.

I finished the job with a deeply satisfied feeling of accomplishment. I had met and surmounted the challenges of the winter woods, using a chainsaw and the sweat of my brow to earn my wages. I'd taken the first determined steps on the forested path I would travel for the next forty years. A path that taught me many lessons of life. One of the first: getting knocked on my ass was one of the surest ways to keep me on my toes.

BILL TORREY is a sixth generation Vermonter who's kin were at Fort Ticonderoga with Ethan Allen in 1775, making his roots deeply attached to the forested hills of the state. He grew up on his family's farmstead in Essex during the 60's and early '70's. By following the rugged heritage of his family, Bill was led to a life working in the woods of Vermont. When he was 19, he was working as a lumberjack earning eighty cents a tree and all the sawdust he could eat.

He soon went off on his own with small, light on the land equipment to better serve the forest and his conscience. His stewardship of the land is regarded as some of the best practiced in the state of Vermont. Bill has supplied certified, sustainably harvested timber on construction projects for the University of Vermont, Middlebury College, The Vermont Maritime Museum, Shelburne Museum, and the Green Mountain Club. In the fall of 2013, Bill retired from logging with most of his sanity and darn near all his fingers and toes.

Bill wrote a monthly column for *Outdoor Magazine* for more than three years. He's been published by the North American Hunting Club and was a member of *The Burlington Free Press* Writer's Group. *Northern Woodlands* magazine solicited an article from him that it plans to publish in an up coming issue.

In the spring of 2014, Bill decided to give oral storytelling a try. He had spent most of his life working alone in the woods, talking mainly to trees, and decided to branch out. He entered five Moth Story Slams in Burlington, winning three. He also won The Vermont Pubic Radio's 2014 Listeners Appreciation Party Story Slam Competition.

In 2015, Bill he entered five Extempo Storytelling Competitions, winning three (www.extempovt.com). He won the December 2015 Moth Story Slam as well. Bill has performed by invitation at The Flynn Theater in Burlington, Middlebury College, The Vermont Folk Life Center, and the Vermont State House.